IRON AGE AND ROMAN(AGRICULTURE IN THE GLOUCESTERSHII SEVERN VALE

edited by Neil Holbrook

PREHISTORIC AND EARLY HISTORIC ACTIVITY, SETTLEMENT AND BURIAL AT WALTON CARDIFF, NEAR TEWKESBURY: EXCAVATIONS AT RUDGEWAY LANE IN 2004–2005

by Jonathan Hart and E.R. McSloy

ROMANO-BRITISH AGRICULTURE AT THE FORMER ST JAMES'S RAILWAY STATION, CHELTENHAM: EXCAVATIONS IN 2000–2001

by Laurent Coleman and Martin Watts

COTSWOLD ARCHAEOLOGY

Bristol and Gloucestershire Archaeological Report No. 6

By agreement with Cotswold Archaeology this report is distributed free
to members of the Bristol and Gloucestershire Archaeological Society
To accompany Volume 126 of the Society's *Transactions* for 2008

Cotswold Archaeology Bristol and Gloucestershire Archaeological Report No. 6

Published by Cotswold Archaeology
© Authors and Cotswold Archaeological Trust Ltd, 2008
Building 11, Kemble Enterprise Park, Cirencester, Gloucestershire GL7 6BQ

All rights reserved. No part of this publication may be reproduced, stored in a retrieval system, or transmitted in any form or by any means, electronic, photocopying, recording or otherwise, without the prior permission of the copyright owner.

ISSN 1479-2389
ISBN 978-0-9553534-3-7

Cotswold Archaeology BAGAR series

1   **A Romano-British and Medieval Settlement Site at Stoke Road, Bishop's Cleeve, Gloucestershire**, by Dawn Enright and Martin Watts, 2002

2   **Later Prehistoric and Romano-British Burial and Settlement at Hucclecote, Gloucestershire**, by Alan Thomas, Neil Holbrook and Clifford Bateman, 2003

3   **Twenty-Five Years of Archaeology in Gloucestershire: a review of new discoveries and new thinking in Gloucestershire, South Gloucestershire and Bristol, 1979–2004**, edited by Neil Holbrook and John Juřica, 2006

4   **Two Cemeteries from Bristol's Northern Suburbs**, edited by Martin Watts, 2006

5   **Prehistoric and Medieval Occupation at Moreton-in-Marsh and Bishop's Cleeve, Gloucestershire**, edited by Martin Watts, 2007

6   **Iron Age and Romano-British Agriculture in the North Gloucestershire Severn Vale**, edited by Neil Holbrook, 2008

Series Editor: Martin Watts
Produced by Past Historic, Kings Stanley, Gloucestershire, GL10 3HW
Printed in Great Britain by Henry Ling Limited, Dorchester, DT1 1HD

FOREWORD

In the last forty years knowledge of the archaeology of the Gloucestershire Severn Valle has increased considerably. A pivotal moment in this process occurred in 1969 when archaeological work associated with the construction of the M5 motorway gave, for the first time, a clear appreciation of the density of sites of all periods present on the claylands. Investigations in the last twenty years in advance of extensive residential developments around such places as Bishop's Cleeve and Tewkesbury have utilised resources out of all proportion to the frantic last gasp rescue work which characterised the M5 project, and the quality of the data retrieved is commensurately better. At Tewkesbury archaeological work between 1991 and 1997 concerned with the construction of the Eastern Relief Road and associated housing developments recovered important information about Bronze Age and Romano-British activity to the south-east of the medieval town. The first site published in this volume enhances the data set reported upon in 2004 in the *Transactions*, and in particular adds information on the Iron Age and Anglo-Saxon periods not represented in the earlier work. In many ways the work at Walton Cardiff has benefited from the lessons learnt on the Eastern Relief Road, the application of extensive geophysical survey proving to be a particularly effective reconnaissance technique. The next wave of archaeological work associated with the major new housing developments destined for the Severn Vale as a consequence of the recently endorsed South-West Regional Spatial Strategy should also build on past achievements, and the sites around Tewkesbury form a benchmark against which to compare and contrast future discoveries.

The second site reported on in this volume was a rare chance to investigate the archaeology of pre-Regency Cheltenham. Slowly the evidence for Romano-British activity beneath the later town is coming to light, although the practicalities of excavating within a thriving modern community are very different to those at green field sites such as Walton Cardiff. The St James's site certainly posed many logistical challenges (for instance the initial evaluation trenches had to be dug through several metres of made ground imported during the construction of the railway station in 1847), but despite the difficulties the results were worthwhile. It is now surely only a matter of time before the settlement to which the excavated Romano-British fieldsystem relates comes to light. We can therefore be confident that much more will be learnt about the field archaeology of the Severn Vale in northern Gloucestershire in the next few years.

Neil Holbrook
Chief Executive, Cotswold Archaeology
December 2008

CONTENTS

ABSTRACTS

Prehistoric and Early Historic Activity, Settlement and Burial at Walton Cardiff

Excavations in 2004–5 at Rudgeway Lane recorded significant remains dating between the mid 2nd millennium BC and the 6th century AD. In the Middle Bronze Age two parallel ditches, *c.* 40m long and 28m apart, were dug. Their interpretation is not straightforward, possibilities include the quarry ditches of a plough-levelled earthen long barrow; two sides of an enclosure or part of a fieldsystem. In the Middle Iron Age a small ditched enclosure, *c.* 25m long by 20m wide with a south-east facing entrance was established on a separate part of the development site. This was superseded in the 1st century AD by an unenclosed settlement comprising a number of roundhouses surrounded by individual drainage ditches which was in turn replaced in the 2nd century AD by a rectilinear ditched enclosure *c.* 105m long by 50m wide with a trackway on its southern side. The enclosure was sub-divided internally to create areas which may have been used for the breeding and folding of stock, the storage and processing of crops and habitation. Structures included a roundhouse, a well and a drying oven. The enclosure continued to be used until the late 3rd century at least, but by then most of the ditches had largely silted up. The latest phase of settlement, which probably dates to the earlier 4th century, was on a much reduced scale from that in the preceding centuries. It is likely that the enclosure was used as part of a mixed farming economy, although pastoralism was probably the dominant activity. Three neonatal burials were associated with the period of unenclosed settlement and at least a further six inhumations were interred in a variety of features within the enclosure. These burials show but one facet of the ritual or superstitious beliefs of the community, which are also reflected in other aspects of the excavated data. In the 6th century two burials were made within the abandoned farmstead, one accompanied by grave goods. They lay close to the line later adopted by a parish boundary, an increasingly recognised pattern in southern England.

Romano-British Agriculture at the Former St James's Railway Station, Cheltenham

Archaeological work between October 1999 and March 2002 revealed a fieldsystem that was used and developed throughout the Roman period, together with a number of pits and postholes. During the late 4th century AD two inhumation burials were interred in the eastern part of the fieldsystem and further ditches and pits were dug. A pit of probable post-Roman date was also found. The settlement with which the fieldsystem was associated probably lies to the north or east of the site.

PREHISTORIC AND EARLY HISTORIC ACTIVITY, SETTLEMENT AND BURIAL AT WALTON CARDIFF, NEAR TEWKESBURY: EXCAVATIONS AT RUDGEWAY LANE IN 2004–2005

by Jonathan Hart and E.R. McSloy

with contributions by
Mary Alexander, Timothy Darvill, Annette Hancocks, Neil Holbrook, Malin Holst,
Emma Tetlow, Fiona Roe, Alan Vince, Sylvia Warman and P.V. Webster

INTRODUCTION
by Jonathan Hart and Annette Hancocks

Over the autumn and winter of 2004–5 Cotswold Archaeology (CA) carried out an arch-aeological excavation at land east of Rudgeway Lane, Walton Cardiff, near Tewkesbury, Gloucestershire, on behalf of Bloor Homes (centred on NGR: SP 9060 3140; Fig. 1). The project was designed to mitigate the archaeological impact of the construction of a new housing estate, the work having been secured by a condition attached to the planning permission.

The parish of Walton Cardiff lies just to the south-east of Tewkesbury within the broad valley of the river Severn in northern Gloucestershire. The steep escarpment of the Cotswold Hills rises from the valley floor 5km to the east of the site and the river Severn itself lies 3.5km to the west. The low-lying ground in and around Tewkesbury is notoriously flood prone, even in modern times, and the development area of 18.4ha lies between the Swilgate and Tirle Brook, minor tributaries of the Severn. The low-lying farmland bordering the watercourses regularly floods during the winter, but the development area occupies an area of slightly raised relief above the 15m AOD contour (Fig. 2). The underlying geology comprises Jurassic Lower Lias Clay and the overlying soils are slowly permeable calcareous clayey soils of the Evesham 2 series (SSEW 1983).

Plans for residential development of the site were first formulated in 1993. Given the discovery nearby of prehistoric and Romano-British sites during work associated with the Tewkesbury Eastern Relief Road, Tewkesbury Borough Council deemed the site to have some archaeological potential. Consequently a programme of fieldwalking and trial trenching was undertaken. The fieldwalking survey revealed a small number of possible prehistoric pot-boilers, but little else which pre-dated the post-medieval period (CAT 1993a). The 1993 evaluation (CAT 1993b) identified a ditch interpreted as a Middle Bronze Age territorial boundary. In 2001 more detailed proposals for development were formulated and a second stage of archaeological evaluation was undertaken. This comprised further evaluation trenches (CA 2002) as well as a magnetometer survey which identified the presence of features consistent with Roman rural settlement (Stratascan 2001). A second magnetometer survey was undertaken in 2004 to complete the coverage of the whole development area (Stratascan 2004). The combined evaluation results showed the site to have clear archaeological potential and so when planning permission was subsequently granted a condition was attached requiring a programme of archaeological work. Initially

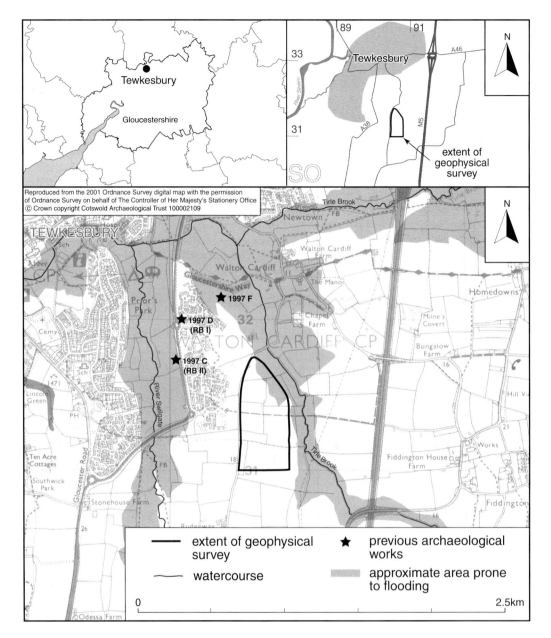

Fig.1: Site location plan (the area shown prone to flooding is based upon information from the Environment Agency website) (scale 1:25000)

it was proposed that the whole of the development area would be stripped of topsoil under archaeological supervision, hand excavation and recording continuing thereafter as appropriate. After the initial phase of topsoil removal had been completed, however, a review of the methodology concluded that the geophysical survey had accurately predicted the extent of significant archaeology, and on that basis the strategy was varied to comprise the excavation of four discrete areas (Fig. 2). Area A contained the two parallel Bronze Age ditches; Areas B and C slight geophysical anomalies, and Area D the Roman rural settlement. Further Iron Age features lay to the south of Area D, beyond the area designated for residential development, although a watching brief was subsequently maintained in this area during the creation of sports pitches.

Fieldwork and post-excavation methodology

Fieldwork commenced with the removal of topsoil and subsoil from the excavation area under constant archaeological supervision using a mechanical excavator equipped with a toothless grading bucket, and continued by hand thereafter. Pits and postholes were subject to a minimum sample of 50% from each feature while structures and features associated with funerary or ritual activity were subject to 100% sample for each feature. It was anticipated originally that ditches would be subject to a minimum sample of 20% for each feature and this methodology was followed throughout the site except in Area D where the well-dated nature of the Roman ditches allowed for a lesser sample to be excavated. In Area A the straightforward stratigraphy meant that relationships between different deposits were identified with a high degree of confidence. This was in contrast to Area D where features assigned to the Roman period were usually filled with homogeneous silts within which stratigraphic relationships were often difficult to determine. A larger degree of difference between the fills of the prehistoric and Roman features was noted and these relationships were established with a high degree of confidence. To the south of Area D the site of two proposed sports pitches was subject to a watching brief in the autumn of 2007 (Fig. 2). The methodology for the construction of these sports pitches was designed to preserve the underlying archaeological deposits *in situ* (CA 2007). Over the general area of the watching brief topsoil stripping was undertaken to a maximum depth of 150mm, thus leaving the subsoil *in situ*, while in the location of the densest concentration of known archaeology no stripping was undertaken. Small quantities of Romano-British pottery as well as post-medieval pottery and clay tobacco pipe stems were recovered from the topsoil but, as intended, no features were exposed. Following completion of the fieldwork an assessment was made of the findings and a strategy proposed for further analysis which has resulted in this publication (CA 2006).

Previous archaeological work in the vicinity of the site

At Tewkesbury, and especially in the suburb of Oldbury, there is limited evidence of intermittent Neolithic and Early Iron Age settlement with more intensive occupation in the Early Roman period, although the full extent of the Roman settlement is still poorly understood (Hannan 1993, 21). Tewkesbury lies on or near the Roman road from Worcester to Gloucester (Margary 1967, Route 180) and coupled with its location at the confluence of two rivers, it is often suggested that there was a small town here.

Archaeological activity to the south-east of Tewkesbury is attested through a series of archaeological investigations undertaken to the west of Rudgeway Lane in advance of housing development and the construction of the Tewkesbury Eastern Relief Road. This work comprised fieldwalking and evaluation (CAT 1991; 1992), followed by excavation centred on three sites, referred to in this text as Sites 1997C (which includes Romano-British Site II), 1997D (including Romano-British Site I) and 1997F (Walker *et al.* 2004; Fig. 1).

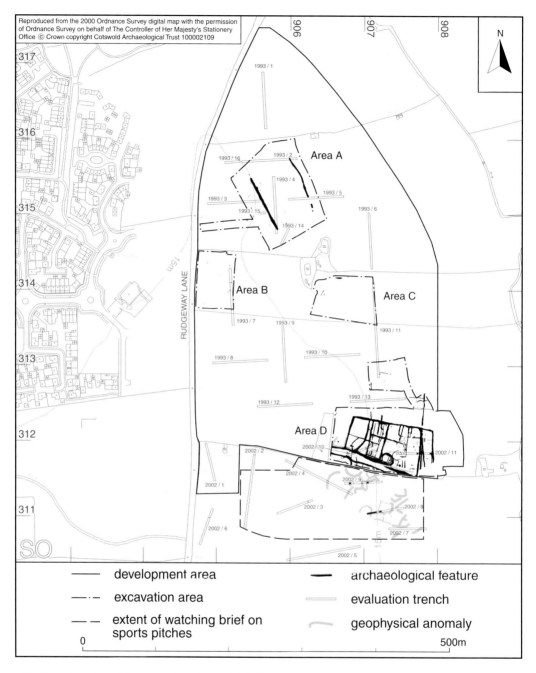

Fig. 2: Location of the excavations (scale 1:5000)

An Early to Middle Bronze Age settlement was identified at Site 1997D, 300m to the north-west of the current site, and similarly located on a slight rise surrounded by low-lying farmland. This settlement comprised a D-shaped enclosure along with ditches and pits and may have been contemporaneous with an area of bronze-casting identified at Site 1997F 150m to its north-east. This casting site appears to reflect a single event of metal production, probably undertaken by itinerant metal workers.

A 2nd-century AD roundhouse and enclosure were found at Site 1997D and may have been broadly contemporaneous with a trackway extending northwards towards the Tirle Brook. This was termed Romano-British Site I. The roundhouse, enclosure and trackway were superseded by a larger sub-rectangular double-ditched enclosure, approximately 65m wide and at least 65m long, dating to the late 2nd to 3rd centuries AD.

Site 1997C (Romano-British Site II) was situated on a similar localised high-spot, 150m to the south of Site 1997D, and here four phases of Romano-British activity were revealed. Phase 1 comprised five curvilinear gullies, some of which may have been roundhouses. These dated from the Late Iron Age/Early Roman period through to the 2nd century. Phase 2 comprised a field system possibly dating to the 2nd century. A major reorganisation of the site occurred during Phase 3 with the creation of a large sub-rectangular enclosure which was subsequently extended and modified to include internal sub-divisions. The southernmost extent of this enclosure was not established but it measured 60m in width by at least 110m in length in its final form. Few internal features were identified within the enclosure although a small number of pits were present. Dating from the enclosure centred on the 2nd to 3rd centuries although the site continued in a changed and much reduced form into the 4th century (Phase 4).

EXCAVATION RESULTS
by Jonathan Hart

Archaeological features and deposits were encountered in excavation Areas A and D only, the geophysical anomalies in Areas B and C proved upon excavation not to have archaeological origins (Fig. 2). A pair of Middle Bronze Age ditches was found in Area A while in Area D features ranged from the Middle Iron Age through to the Anglo-Saxon period. The excavated features have been assigned the following chronological periods, with distinct phases of activity discernible within Period 4:

Period 1: Middle Bronze Age (mid 2nd millennium BC) (Area A)
Period 2: Middle Iron Age (*c.* 4th to 2nd century BC) (Area D)
Period 3: Late Iron Age/Early Roman (*c.* 1st century AD) (Area D)
Period 4: Roman (1st to 4th centuries AD) (Area D)
Period 5: Anglo-Saxon (6th century AD) (Area D)

Features dating to the post-medieval and modern periods were associated with the recent agricultural history of the site and are not discussed below. A series of post-medieval east/west aligned furrows were identified throughout the excavation area, but to increase clarity these have been omitted from the plans.

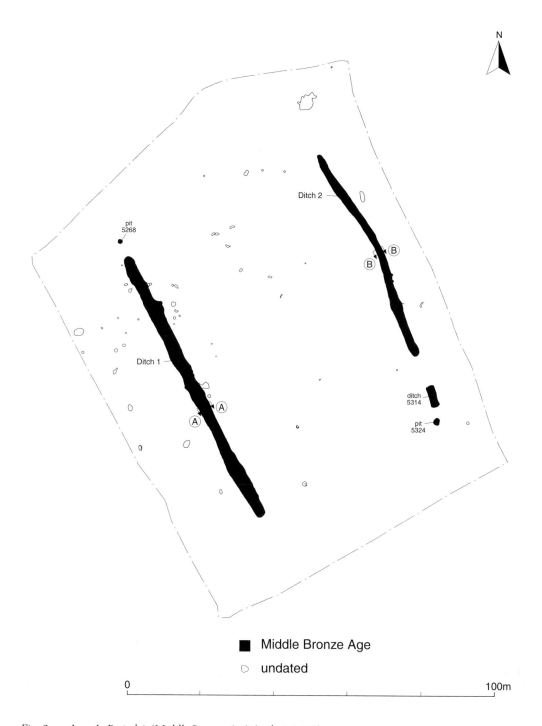

Fig. 3:   *Area A, Period 1 (Middle Bronze Age) (scale 1:1000)*

Period 1: Middle Bronze Age (mid 2nd millennium BC) (Fig. 3)

Two parallel north-west/south-east aligned ditches *c.* 28m apart were found: Ditch 1 38m long, with a pit, 5268, near its north-western terminal; Ditch 2 30m long with a further 3m length of ditch, 5314, and a pit, 5324, beyond its south-eastern terminal. The profiles of the ditches varied but both were up to 3.4m wide and 1.4m deep becoming shallower towards their terminals. Both ditches were steep sided with a U- to slightly V-shaped profile (Fig. 4). Occasional steps in the ditch profiles might reflect recutting: this is apparent in Fig. 4, section AA where fill 5359 may be the only remaining fill of the primary cut of Ditch 1.

Ditch 1: section AA

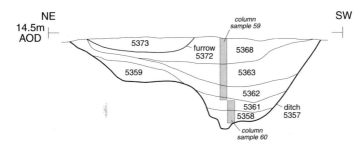

Ditch 2: section BB

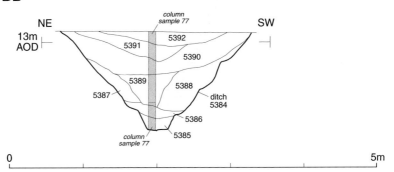

Fig. 4:   Area A, Ditches 1 and 2, sections AA and BB (scale 1:50)

The ditches contained similar fill sequences and analysis of column samples indicated that these accumulated as a result of erosion along the cut edges and of fluvial or aeolian transportation (Green and Branch 2006, 82–4, fig. 4). A few of the fills also contained moderate quantities of stones, perhaps the only evidence for the former presence of a bank. The animal bone included both domestic and wild taxa: cattle, sheep/goat, pig, dog and red deer. All of the bone was highly weathered and much had been gnawed by dogs, suggesting that it had been exposed prior to deposition. Small quantities of Middle Bronze Age pottery were recovered from the two ditches along with a tanged arrowhead of similar date from Ditch 1 (Fig.13). Radiocarbon dates obtained from carbonised residues on pottery from Ditch 1 dated to 1530–1410 cal. BC and 1440–1290 cal. BC at 95.4% confidence level (Wk-20711 and Wk-21274) and confirmed the Middle Bronze Age date (Table 13).

Ditch 5314 and pits 5268 and 5324 lay on an extension of the ditch alignments. Ditch 5314 was shallower than Ditch 2 and contained a very different fill of dark, waste-rich material containing animal bone and Middle Bronze Age pottery. Pit 5324 appeared to form the southernmost extent of this alignment, although it remained undated. In a similar manner pit 5268 probably formed the northernmost extent of the Ditch 1 alignment.

Period 2: Middle Iron Age (c. 4th to 2nd century BC) (Fig. 5)

Enclosure 1 was sub-rectangular, *c.* 25m long by 20m wide, with an entrance halfway along its eastern length. The ditch was 1.0–1.4m wide and 0.4m deep. A fragment of human femur was recovered from its fill. While the enclosure may have been open-sided to the south, it is more likely that the ditch was destroyed by the Roman trackway ditch on this side of the enclosure. Two undated ditch sections (5980 and 6047) exposed beneath the trackway ditch might be associated with the only surviving vestiges of it (Fig. 5; section CC). If this is the case a length of ditch to the south of the enclosure either served for drainage or else defined an annex or boundary. No internal features were found within the enclosure, which is poorly dated by small quantities of pottery, including one Middle Iron Age sherd. Since the enclosure is stratigraphically earlier than features assigned to Period 3 a Middle Iron Age date is suggested.

Period 3: Late Iron Age/Early Roman (c. 1st century AD) (Fig. 6)

Late Iron Age activity was centred on the highest part of the site. The pottery assemblage from the Period 3 features dates broadly to the 1st century AD and the presence of wheel-thrown 'Belgic' style vessels, Severn Valley ware and two Aucissa brooches, recovered as residual finds from Period 4 ditches (see Fig. 17, nos 1 and 2), indicates that activity extended into the post-Conquest period.

The westernmost extent of the site was defined by a series of ditches (Ditches 3, 4, 5 and 6) between 1 and 2m wide and 0.5m deep. Ditch 4 was a recut of Ditch 3. A gap between Ditches 3/4 and Ditches 5/6 was centred on the high point of the rise and created a funnel-shaped entrance. The ditches were largely filled by dark silts containing moderate quantities of pottery, animal bone, fired and burnt clay fragments and burnt stone.

Activity to the east of this boundary comprised two enclosures (2 and 3) and a small number of pits, postholes and ditches. A ring ditch lay further to the north. Enclosure 2 comprised a sub-rectangular area of *c.* 17m long by 11m wide and defined by insubstantial ditches with opposing entrances on a south-east/north-west axis. The southern perimeter of the enclosure appeared to have been truncated by a later trackway ditch, although it is possible that the enclosure was open along this side. The perimeter ditch around Enclosure 2 was filled with pale-coloured silts which contained few finds except in the south-western corner where the fills were darker and contained pottery, animal bone and possible loom weight fragments. Posthole 5978, just outside the western entrance to this enclosure, contained the base of a pottery vessel.

Two undated parallel ditches, 6188 and 6401, may have been associated with Enclosure 2 since they appeared to respect its location and were stratigraphically earlier than the

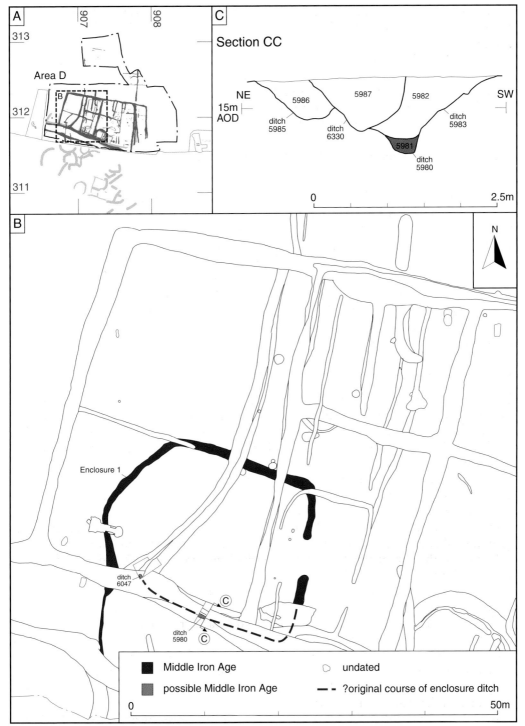

Fig. 5:   Area D, Period 2 (Middle Iron Age) (scale 1:500). Section CC (scale 1:50)

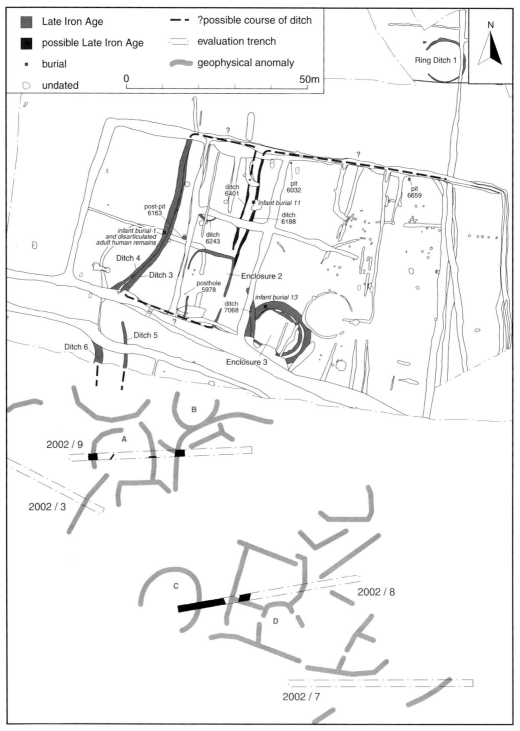

Fig. 6:   Area D, Period 3 (1st century AD) (scale 1:1000)

later Roman ditches. These ditches extended northwards from the enclosure and, if contemporary with one another, might have defined a double-ditched boundary or narrow droveway. Like much of the enclosure perimeter these ditches contained limited dating evidence. Ditches 3/4 and 6401 and 6188 all terminated beneath the northern perimeter ditch of the later (Period 4) Enclosure 4. Similarly pits 6659 and 6032 to the east lay just inside the line of that perimeter ditch. It is simplest to assume that Ditches 3/4, 6401 and 6188 defined an enclosure or paddock, the northern side of which had been destroyed by the creation of Enclosure 4. If this is correct Ditch 6 may have formed an agricultural boundary to the south, separated by the entrance gap with Ditch 3/4.

Enclosure 3 lay to the east of Enclosure 2 and was of ovoid plan between 8 and 12m in diameter. It was defined by two concentric ditches which showed some evidence of recutting. The broader outer ditch was later than the much narrower inner ditch and may have been a recut. Two elongated scoops excavated into the base of the outer ditch contained Burial 13, the flexed inhumation of a neonate, and the upper part of a carinated bowl dating to the mid to late 1st century AD (see Fig. 15, no. 18). The lower part of the same bowl was recovered from another part of the outer ditch. It is likely that Enclosure 3 was a drainage ditch surrounding the site of a roundhouse and both ditches contained similar fills and finds to those of Enclosure 2. Ditch 7068, which cut Enclosure 3, contained Late Iron Age to 1st-century AD pottery. It is unclear whether this represents a late sub-phase within Period 3 or whether it dates to Period 4. Two further neonates were buried in the latest fills of other ditches. Burial 1 was interred in the top of Ditch 4 and was associated with 1st/2nd-century AD pottery and disarticulated adult human remains. Burial 11 was placed within a pit dug into the fill of Ditch 6188. It is unclear whether these burials date to the end of Period 3 or the start of Period 4.

Few other features could be ascribed confidently to this period. Ditch 6243, a shallow curvilinear gully, was truncated by later ditches and was very poorly defined. Post-pit 6163, complete with post-packing and post-pipe, truncated a smaller undated pit. Animal bone, fired clay lumps and pottery were recovered from its backfill. Pits 6032 and 6659 were shallow scoop-like features from which small amounts of pottery and bone were recovered.

Ring Ditch 1, which probably served as a drip gully surrounding a roundhouse, was located to the north of the other features and was stratigraphically earlier than a Roman field system. It was 11m in diameter with a narrow U-shaped profile and an irregular base, and was between 0.25 and 0.8m wide and between 0.05 and 0.22m deep. A gap within the western part of the circuit may have been an entrance or else simply the result of truncation. The ring ditch was filled with silts containing small quantities of animal bone, fired clay and Late Iron Age to 1st-century AD pottery. A larger concentration of cow and sheep long bones was recovered from a dark upper fill (5796) close to the possible entrance. Two undated postholes (5712 and 5714; not illustrated) just outside the possible entrance may have been associated with the structure.

The area to the south of the main excavation was subject to geophysical survey and evaluation trenching (CA 2002). The geophysical survey detected at least four curvilinear anomalies which were of similar dimensions to Enclosure 3 and presumably also mark the site of roundhouses within an otherwise unenclosed settlement (Fig. 6, A–D). The geophysical survey extended for 90m south of the area shown on Fig. 6 with largely negative results. It is therefore likely that that the true extent of the settlement has been detected. Enclosure A was sampled by evaluation trench 2002/9 and Enclosure C by trench 2002/8. The earliest ditch of Enclosure A did not contain any dating evidence but the recut yielded 19 sherds of Malvernian rock-tempered and limestone-tempered pottery. To the east of this, a curvilinear ditch produced pottery of a similar date. The ditch of Enclosure C produced 78 sherds of pottery, principally Malvernian limestone-tempered with lesser quantities of Malvernian rock-tempered and one sherd of grog tempered ware; three joining sherds of Droitwich briquetage, animal bones and numerous burnt pebbles. The rectilinear enclosure to the east produced pottery of a similar date. The dating evidence recovered from the evaluation trenches demonstrates that these features can be ascribed to Period 3.

Period 4: Roman (1st to 4th centuries AD)

The dominant activity within Area D dated to the Roman period and was once again focused on the high point in the local topography exploited in Periods 2 and 3. Period 4 has been sub-divided into three phases on the basis of stratigraphic and ceramic evidence, although the pottery was typically conservative in nature, a common trait of rural assemblages in the region. Most of the pottery was recovered from ditches with a high risk of residuality. Severn Valley wares provided some limited indicators of date with more specific date markers provided largely by non-local wares including samian, Dorset Black-burnished wares and Oxfordshire products. A very small assemblage of metal objects was recovered, including coins, brooches, nails and miscellaneous objects, but was of limited use for dating purposes.

Phase 4a (1st to 2nd centuries AD)

Phase 4a is represented by three ditches (Fig. 7). Ditches 6187 and 6637 comprised two early cuts of a drainage ditch which during Phase 4b formed the northern side of a trackway. Ditch 6187 is undated but is stratigraphically one of the earliest cuts of the trackway ditches. In contrast, ditch 6637 contained dark-coloured fills which produced animal bone and 1st/2nd-century AD pottery. One of the lowest fills of this ditch contained a deliberately structured deposit, comprising the complete rim of a Severn Valley ware vessel and an upright and almost entire large-necked Severn Valley ware jar sealed by a dump of redeposited natural clay.

Ditch 6400 was a short L-shaped ditch within a later enclosure dating to Phase 4b. Although this ditch contained pottery dating to the Late Iron Age to 1st/2nd centuries AD, and conceivably originated in Phase 4a, it probably continued in use into Phase 4b. A fragment of bird bone fashioned into a whistle or flute was recovered from one of its fills.

Phase 4b (2nd to late 3rd or early 4th century AD)

The majority of activity in Area D could be dated to the 2nd to 3rd centuries AD (Fig. 7). The Phase 4a drainage ditch 6637/6187 was recut and a parallel ditch added to the south to form a trackway 5.5–8.0m wide. No surfaces survived between the ditches which had been recut on a number of occasions before finally silting up. The southern ditch was filled by relatively light-coloured silts and contrasted with the northern ditch which contained fills that became progressively darker and more finds rich towards the central area of the site. Within this finds-rich zone, large quantities of 2nd/3rd-century AD pottery, animal bone and burnt clay were recovered as well as a fragment of a Colchester-derivative brooch

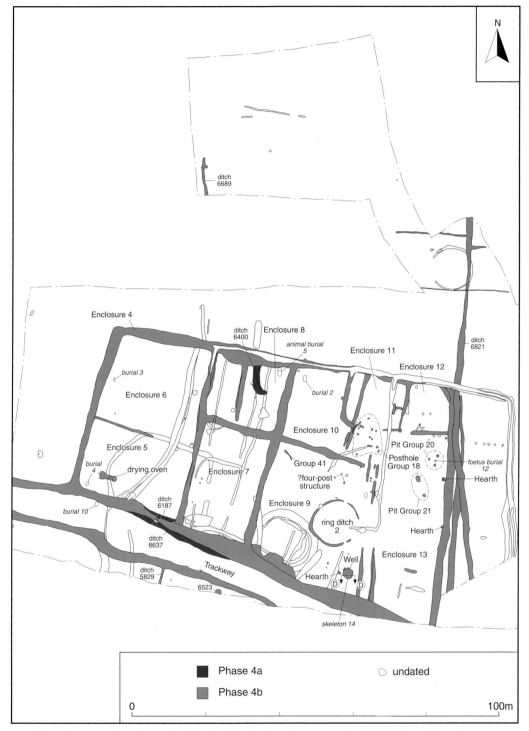

Fig. 7:   *Area D, Phases 4a and 4b (2nd to late 3rd or 4th century AD) (scale 1:1000)*

dateable to the later 1st to 2nd centuries AD (Fig. 17, no. 3). The jaw and skull of an adult horse were recovered from the base of one of the recuts of the northern trackway ditch.

The trackway was adjoined along its northern side by Enclosure 4, of sub-rectangular plan 105m long by 50m wide, defined by a substantial ditch. There was no discernible entrance to this enclosure, although one may have been obscured by modern truncation at its south-eastern corner, or access may have been afforded via timber bridges. Enclosure 4 was sub-divided by large ditches into a grid pattern of seven sub-enclosures (Enclosures 5–10 and 13). Finds from the perimeter ditch of Enclosure 4 ditch included an iron double-spiked loop, a fragment from a snake's head terminal pennanular bracelet (Fig. 17, no. 5) and a quern or millstone fragment. Localised dumps of cobble-sized stones and burnt and unburnt roof tiles and nails were found within the easternmost perimeter ditches. Very small amounts of ceramic building material were recovered, and there were no dense concentrations of building material (a small cluster of such material from the ditches defining Enclosures 11 and 12 was too slight to suggest a building at this location).

Few of the sub-enclosures contained internal features. Notable exceptions comprise a drying oven within Enclosure 5, a ring ditch (2) with a possible four-post structure, a hearth and a well within Enclosure 9, and a group of hearths, a few pits and a burial within Enclosure 13. The drying oven in Enclosure 5 was poorly preserved (Fig. 8). It was keyhole shaped, 4.6m long, including a 1.45m diameter stokehole at its eastern end. Parts of a pitched stone lining, 5816 and 5817, survived along the flue. The clay substrate along the flue and within the stokehole had been scorched and the oven was filled with dark charcoal-rich deposits 5663 and 5697 (not illustrated). Pottery dating to the 2nd to 4th centuries and part of a late 3rd/4th-century twisted wire bracelet were recovered from fill 5663. After these fills had accumulated the oven was re-used or robbed, evidenced by a cut 5818 (not illustrated) which was dug deep enough to expose the walls of the oven which

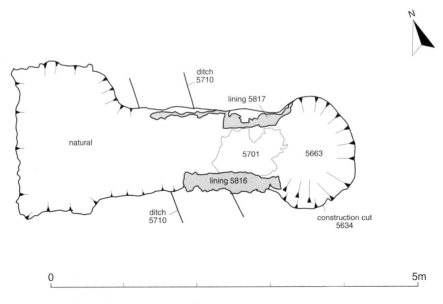

Fig. 8:   *Plan of drying oven 1 (scale 1:50)*

might then have been re-used as a fire pit. The cut was backfilled with demolition material 5701 and 5635, presumably derived from the structure of either the original oven or its successor. Fill 5701 contained 2nd to 3rd-century pottery. The remnant hollow left by this partial backfilling was filled with topsoil 5662 from which 4th-century pottery and a coin dating to AD 330–5 were recovered.

Enclosure 9 appears to have been the focus of domestic activity within Enclosure 4 as it contained a roundhouse (Ring Ditch 2), a possible four-post structure, a hearth and a well. These features all yielded pottery consistent with a 2nd to 4th-century AD date. The northern edge of the trackway ditch had been eroded at this point, possibly as a result of trampling, to form a broad, shallow lip alongside the enclosure and this may define the location of a bridged entrance. A burnt fragment from a quern or millstone was recovered from the westernmost ditch of this enclosure.

Ring Ditch 2 was an interrupted ditch 10m in diameter which is likely to have been the drip gully surrounding a roundhouse. Some of the breaks within the circuit were the result of truncation, although on its eastern side a gap up to 6m long, while at least partially a product of truncation, might mark the site of an entrance. The ditch was variously filled with both light-coloured silts and darker finds-rich fills which contained animal bone, a few iron nails, a fragment of bottle glass and part of a copper-alloy pennanular bracelet (see Fig. 17, no. 4). The last two items were both of 2nd/3rd-century AD date.

The possible four-post structure in fact comprised only three postholes forming an L-shaped alignment. However, all of the postholes were shallow and it is conceivable that a fourth posthole had originally existed. A small pit, its natural clay walls scorched red by burning, evidently served as a hearth. No associated deposits survived and it is unclear whether it had a domestic or an industrial function.

The well was built by digging a construction cone (6793), 3m in diameter at its top, which contained a 0.7m diameter stone-lined shaft (6789) reaching a depth of 4.5m (Figs 9 and 10). A very soft silt (7144) at the base of the well contained a large insect assemblage,

Fig. 9: The well under excavation

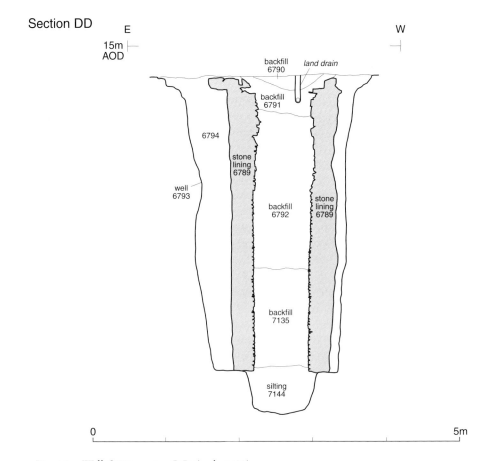

Fig. 10: Well 6789, section DD (scale 1:50)

suggesting that it accumulated over an extended period while the well remained in use (see *the insect remains*, below). This deposit also contained large quantities of pottery, including a minimum of six substantially complete Severn Valley ware vessels and a costrel, all with fresh breaks suggesting either that they were lost during use or were deliberate placements (see Fig. 16, nos 38–40). A socketed iron object (see Fig. 18) recovered from this fill may have been a boat hook, thatching tool or weapon adapted for the retrieval of lost buckets from the well. Animal bone from 7144 comprised material from one cow, at least one sheep, at least two sheep/goat, one pig, one dog/fox, one field vole, one vole sp., one blackbird/thrush, at least 12 frogs, one toad and four frog/toad. The sheep bones included a front limb from a single individual, and only the cattle tibia showed signs of butchery. The primary silting was sealed by a number of sequential backfills, the lowest of which (7135) may also have accumulated during the life of the well. This contained the human skeleton (SK 14) of a young adult male who had suffered from lung infections which were healing at the time of death and large quantities of animal bones deriving from at least three cattle, two horses, two goats, four sheep, three sheep/goat, and a pig as well as rodents and frogs/toads. Although a minimum of four individual sheep were present, the majority of the bones were from two partial skeletons of a juvenile and a sub-adult. Significant parts of three fox skeletons were also present. Like the sheep these are very well preserved and show no signs of butchery. The sheep and fox carcasses must have been deposited rapidly with flesh still attached, evidenced by the lack of weathering and gnawing marks and the high degree of articulation.

Backfill 7135 was overlain by 6792, a dump of stones likely to have derived from the demolition of the upstanding part of the well structure, which contained horse and cattle bones (the latter had been butchered). Above this were two dumps of redeposited topsoil, 6790 and 6791, containing butchered and weathered cattle and horse bones and abraded 3rd-century AD pottery. Three postholes adjacent to the well might have formed part of the superstructure. Three further postholes located on an arc separating the well from Ring Ditch 2 may have supported a fence line forming a physical barrier between the well and the roundhouse.

Three hearths and two pit groups were found within Enclosure 13. The hearths were shallow oval pits with scorched edges that had been partially cut into the final fill of the easternmost perimeter ditch. This ditch had been recut further to the east and it is possible that the hearths were sheltered by a bank associated with the recut. None contained material suitable for determining their function. Pit Group 20 comprised a shallow oval pit containing a flexed inhumation of a late term foetus (SK 12) surrounded by three similarly sized pits. There were no special depositions within the satellite pits and it is possible that they formed part of a boundary or structure marking the burial. Pit Group 21 comprised two shallow, scoop-like pits with dark fills from which small amounts of animal bone and pottery were recovered. Within Enclosures 8 and 10 more ditches served to further sub-divide these spaces.

The north-eastern corner of Enclosure 4 was modified by the creation of two further enclosures (Enclosures 11 and 12). These were small sub-rectangular ditched enclosures measuring 15m by 13m and 12m by 12m respectively. Each had a south-facing entrance, that into Enclosure 11 was 7m wide, although it may have been narrower given the presence of Posthole Group 18 discussed below, while the entrance into Enclosure 12 was 2.75m wide. The stratigraphic relationships between the ditches of these enclosures and those of Enclosure 4 demonstrated that all functioned contemporaneously. The ditches of both enclosures had fills from which moderate to large quantities of animal bone and pottery were recovered along with moderate quantities of medium-sized stones. There was a cluster of 18 postholes within and to the immediate south of the entrance to Enclosure 11. Although it was difficult to determine any meaningful patterns it is possible that they formed part of a fence line extending south from the enclosure entrance. Other occasional isolated pits and postholes were distributed throughout Enclosure 4 but there were no other recognisable groupings.

A number of human burials were associated with Enclosure 4. Burial 2, the flexed inhumation of a middle-aged male, lay in a corner of Enclosure 10. Six iron nails found around the edges of the cut suggested interment in a wooden coffin. The left femur of the burial was radiocarbon dated to between 50 cal. BC–350 cal. AD at 95% confidence level (Wk-21277). Four other burials have been assigned to this phase (Burials 3, 4, 5 and 10) because, although strictly they are undated, like Burial 2 they were all located adjacent to the perimeter ditch of Enclosure 4. Burials 2, 4 and 5 were in placed at the corners of enclosures. Burial 3 was almost entirely truncated by ploughing but enough survived to determine that it was that of an adult male within a north/south aligned grave. Burials 4 and 10 were flexed inhumations of middle-aged males placed within oval north-east/ south-west aligned grave cuts. Burial 4 was interred with the head to the north and the body facing east while Burial 10 was placed with the head to the south and the body facing west. This man exhibited damage to the skull probably resulting from blunt force trauma, although he had survived this injury. A shell and a pebble were present within the grave fill of Burial 10 but might be incidental components of the grave fill rather than deliberate placements. Burial 5 was unusual in that it comprised a grave-sized sub-rectangular cut with two postholes in the base. This contained no human skeleton, the empty grave being backfilled with a silty clay on top of which a sheep had been interred.

The only Romano-British features exposed outside Enclosure 4 were ditches 6821 and 6689 to the north of the enclosure and ditch 5829 to its south. These were slighter than most of the ditches that comprised Enclosure 4 and were filled with light coloured silts from which few finds were recovered. A further pit or ditch terminus, 6523, was present to the south of the southernmost trackway ditch but extended beyond the limit of excavation.

Phase 4c (late 3rd to 4th centuries AD)

A small number of features were found that were stratigraphically later than those of Phase 4b or which contained artefacts dateable to the late 3rd to 4th centuries AD (Fig. 11). Although it was clear that most of the Phase 4b ditches had at least partially silted up by this time, the fact that they were respected by the Phase 4c ditches and the later finds which derived from their upper fills demonstrates that they continued to be visible into Phase 4c. Late activity is also evidenced through the presence of a coin of AD 330–5 and a fragment of a cable bracelet dateable to the 4th century recovered from the infilling of the drying oven.

Enclosure 4 was extended a further 13m eastwards by ditches 7011 and 7067. A fragment of a copper-alloy strip bracelet was recovered from a fill of ditch 7067 (see Fig. 17, no. 6). Ditch 6774 was cut into the partially silted northern ditch of Enclosure 4 and returned for a short distance on its western side recutting the ditch which had separated Enclosures 6 and 8. A third ditch, 6504, extended south from the perimeter ditch beyond the western terminal of ditch 7067 confirming that the Phase 4b ditches were still visible earthworks. Ditches 6184 and 6504 were far slighter than the Phase 4b ditches and it is possible that they had been more heavily truncated. While the plan of Phase 4c features may therefore well be incomplete, ditches 6184 and 6504 do define a sub-rectangular enclosure *c.* 47m by 37m in area with a further enclosure adjoining to the east and bounded by ditches 7011 and 7067.

An alignment of postholes (Group 22) lay just inside ditch 6774. It is possible that the former eastern perimeter of Enclosure 4 survived as an earthwork and that these postholes defined a small enclosure in the north-eastern corner of the extension. Two further features can be ascribed to this phase: pit 6382, located just inside the possible enclosure defined by ditches 6184 and 6504 and ditch 6706 which extended north-eastwards from the trackway. The alignment of ditch 6706 was unusual but it is possible that the trackway ditch survived as an earthwork into which ditch 6706 drained.

The fills of the Phase 4c ditches were typically pale deposits containing little dateable material. Ditch 6504 contained a large proportion of the later pottery assemblage including Oxfordshire colour-coated ware, whiteware mortaria, Malvernian wares, late forms in Dorset Black-burnished ware and late imitation Black-burnished ware. A single sherd of

Fig. 11: Area D, Phase 4c (late 3rd or 4th century AD) (scale 1:1000)

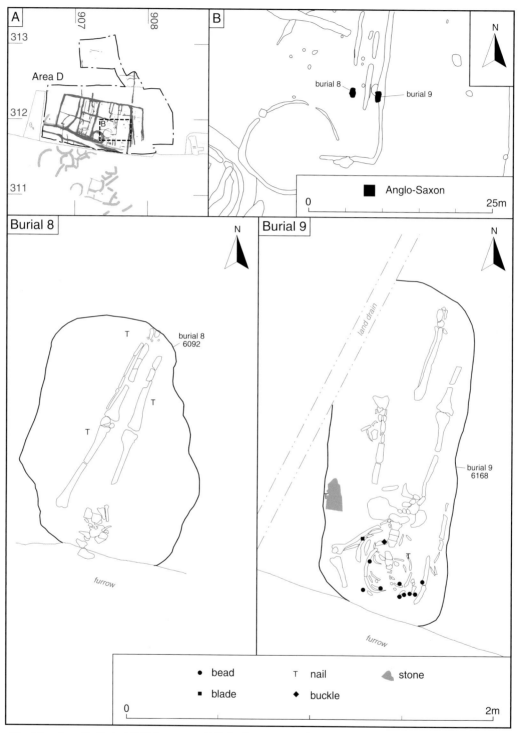

Fig. 12: Area D, Period 5 (6th century AD) (scales 1:500 and 1:20)

shell-tempered ware recovered may date to the second half of the 4th century AD. Ditch 7067 also contained a few localised dumps of darker material which included animal bone, pottery, burnt clay and charcoal. The final deposit within the Roman site was a fine mollusc-rich silt which formed the uppermost fill of the northern and eastern perimeter ditches of Enclosure 4 and is further indication that much of the enclosure survived as an earthwork into Phase 4c.

Period 5: Anglo-Saxon (6th century AD) (Fig. 12)

Inhumation burials 8 and 9 post-dated the Romano-British farmstead and the grave goods accompanying Burial 9 show that they date to the 6th century AD. Both had been truncated by furrows which had removed the upper parts of the bodies. The burials were laid side by side on a north/south alignment with the feet to the north. Burial 8 was an extended inhumation of a middle-aged male; the shape of the grave cut was impossible to reconstruct due to the level of truncation. Burial 9 was more complete although the skull was missing, and was contained within a sub-rectangular grave, cut into Phase 4c ditch 6504. It contained the extended inhumation of a middle-aged female accompanied by grave goods comprising a glass and amber bead necklace, an iron knife, and an iron belt buckle and plate (see Fig. 19). Iron nails were found with both burials, and those associated with Burial 8 were located around the circumference of the cut, suggesting that one or both inhumations had been interred in a coffin. Other finds within the grave fills consisted of Roman pottery and animal bone but the poor preservation of the latter suggests both classes of finds were residual.

Period 6: undated (not illustrated)

A few undated features were found throughout Areas A and D. Those in Area A all appeared to be of natural origin and were probably tree-throw pits. Those in Area D comprised a small number of pits and postholes as well as ditch 6471.

THE FINDS
by E.R. McSloy with contributions by Fiona Roe, Alan Vince and P.V. Webster

The worked flint

A total of 45 pieces of worked flint weighing 261g was recovered, 16 from Period 1 Middle Bronze Age deposits in Area A, the remainder from Period 3 and 4 deposits in Area D or else unstratified (Table 1). The worked flint from Area D occurred largely in association with Late Iron Age and later ceramics and can be considered to be redeposited.

The condition of the flint is generally good with few pieces exhibiting extensive edge damage or rolling. The majority of pieces are patinated, resulting in partial or overall white discolouration. The raw material consists of dark grey and buff-brown coloured flint of variable quality. The poor quality of some of the assemblage suggests that it derived from secondary (gravel) sources, although the small number of flakes retaining patches of thick, chalky cortex do indicate use of material from primary sources (chalk or chalk soil).

Table 1: Quantification of the worked flint by period

Type	Period 1	Periods 3–4/us	Total	Mean weight (g)
	Count	*Count*		
Flake/chip (primary)	–	1	1	6
Flake/chip (secondary)	4	10	14	4.7
Flake/chip (tertiary)	8	10	18	3.9
Core frag.	1	1	2	7.5
Fabricator	–	1	1	30
Piercer	–	1	1	16
Scraper	1	2	3	10.3
Retouched flake	1	2	3	5.7
Arrowhead leaf	–	1	1	5
Arrowhead tanged	1	–	1	3
Total	**16**	**29**	**45**	

Flake removals from across the site are of similar type, characteristically broad and squat and predominantly secondary or tertiary. Most appear uncontrolled with no evidence for platform preparation or selection.

The group associated with Middle Bronze Age features (Ditches 1 and 2) in Area A consists mainly of unutilised flakes and is indistinct compositionally from the remainder of the assemblage. A single tool, a crudely made tanged arrowhead from Ditch 1, fill 5392 (Fig. 13), is of Early to Middle Bronze Age date and as such is consistent with the date of the associated pottery. Dateable pieces from the remainder of the assemblage are restricted to a fabricator of Late Neolithic/Early Bronze Age date (unstratified) and a leaf arrowhead of earlier Neolithic date which was a residual find in Phase 4c.

Although the number of tools represented is fewer, the worked flint compares in other respects with material from the Eastern Relief Road sites (Tingle 2004, 57–9). The limited incidence of primary flakes and core/core fragments apparent in both groups indicates that the flint-working that was taking place in the area may have taken the form of manufacture or upkeep of flake tools, with primary reduction taking place elsewhere.

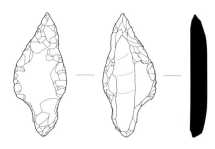

0   50mm

Fig. 13: Flint arrowhead (scale 1:1)

The prehistoric pottery

The pottery was sorted into fabric groups defined on the basis of the dominant inclusions present, and fabric types based on inclusion size, abundance or other characteristics (PCRG 1997). Identification was primarily by macroscopic observation in some instances assisted by a (x10 power) binocular microscope. The pottery was recorded by sherd count and weight for each fabric type by context and minimum vessel number (sherd families). Vessel form was recorded for featured sherds. In addition, wall thickness ranges, surface treatment and any evidence of use were recorded. The assemblage was recorded using an MS Access database, a copy of which is contained in the archive.

Representative samples of fabric types were selected for thin-section analysis and the results incorporated into this report. Analysis of fabric MALV was undertaken in an effort to determine its source more precisely and to establish any link between this and visibly similar Iron Age fabrics. A grog-tempered sherd was included in an effort to confirm or refute a non-local source.

Period 1: Middle Bronze Age (mid 2nd millennium BC)

A small assemblage amounting to 162 sherds (1144g), representing a minimum of 82 vessels, can be ascribed to this period. The majority of this material was recovered from Ditches 1 and 2 in Area A, further sherds occurring residually in Area D. The 33 sherds of Middle Bronze Age and Beaker pottery recovered from the earlier evaluation of Ditches 1 and 2 has not been further considered here (Timby 2004a, 59–62).

With the exception of six sherds (6g) retrieved following sorting of material from bulk soil sample residues, the Bronze Age pottery was hand collected. Average sherd weight was low at 7.7g and this is a good reflection of the fragmented nature of the assemblage. Occasional sherds (e.g. Fig. 14, no. 3) are larger, enabling the reconstruction of the (upper) profile of a vessel.

Fabrics (incorporating summary comments on thin-section analysis by Alan Vince)
The larger part of the Bronze Age assemblage (Table 2) comprised material in fabric MALV which is characterised by coarse igneous/metamorphic rock inclusions derived from a Malvernian source. The fabric is visibly similar, though perhaps coarser, to well-known Middle Iron Age Malvernian fabrics from the region (Peacock 1968).

Table 2: Quantification of the Middle Bronze Age pottery by sherd count (c), minimum number of vessels (mv) and weight (w; in grammes)

	Fabric	MALV	GROG	ORG	QZ	SH	Totals
Area	**Feature**	c/mv/w	c/mv/w	c/mv/w	c/mv/w	c/mv/w	c/mv/w
A	Ditch 1	54/40/571	1/1/18	–	–	–	**55/41/589**
	Ditch 2	54/17/179	–	4/2/9	1/1/4	19/6/120	**78/26/312**
	Other	12/5/55	–	–	–	2/1/15	**14/6/70**
D	Various, P. 3/4	11/6/153	4/3/20	–	–	–	**15/9/173**
	Totals	*131/68/958*	*5/4/38*	*4/2/9*	*1/1/4*	*21/7/135*	*162/82/1144*

MALVERNIAN COARSE 'ROCK'-TEMPERED (MALV)

Handmade. Coarser rock inclusions up to 7mm may protrude from the surfaces and include hornblend-gneiss, quartz-mica schist, fine-grained basic dolerite, gneiss, hornblend-granite, altered rhyolite, quartz-epidote schist, rounded quartz, and sandstone. Inclusions range in size from *c.* 0.2mm to 3mm. Hard-fired with sandy surface feel and irregular fracture. Dark grey throughout or with red-brown exterior surface.

GROG-TEMPERED (GROG)

Handmade. Grog inclusions are self-coloured or darker grey and up to 3mm. The following inclusion types were noted in thin-section: quartz, sub-angular and rounded up to 5mm; limestone, rounded and angular up to 5mm across; grog, angular, voids up to 5mm and of similar size to the limestone inclusions; organics. Soft, with soapy feel and irregular fracture. Mid-brown surfaces with grey core.

ORGANIC (ORG)

Handmade. Common plate-like and linear voids visible in breaks and at surfaces (2–4mm); also sparse limestone and quartz inclusions. Soft, with soapy feel and irregular fracture. Patchy grey/mid brown surfaces with dark grey core.

QUARTZ (QZ)

Handmade. Common quartz and medium/fine (0.5–1mm) igneous/metamorphic rock inclusions. Hard, with sandy feel and finely irregular fracture. Dark grey throughout.

SPARSE FOSSIL SHELL (SH)

Rare coarse fossil shell inclusions up to 4mm and rare inclusions which are self-coloured or darker grey and up to 3mm. Hard with soapy feel and irregular fracture. It differs from the later prehistoric shelly type fabric with patchy brown/grey exterior surfaces with grey core and interior. It matches the description for Fabric P8 (Timby 2004a, 60).

Discussion by Alan Vince

Malvernian coarse 'rock'-tempered (MALV)

The wide range of rock types present and the evidence for their being a natural breccia rather than humanly prepared temper points conclusively to a source for this fabric in the Malvern Hills area. The source can be localised closely because of the distinctive geology of the area. The rounded quartz grains are ultimately of Triassic origin but are the main component of Severn terrace sands. These only occur on the eastern side of the Malvern Hills, allowing a source to the west of the hills to be excluded. The source of the rock inclusions can be pinpointed to the southern part of the Hills since the sample contains rhyolite, which occurs in the pre-Cambrian Warren House group, which outcrops on the eastern side of Herefordshire Beacon, and a quartz sandstone, which only occurs in the Malvern Hills in isolated inliers of Cambrian rocks in the Midsummer Hill/Hollybush Hill area and as a major exposure on the south-west side of the hills. The only area where all these rock types outcrop close together is between Herefordshire Beacon and Midsummer Hill and therefore the source of the pottery clay must lie in the block of land bounded by Little Malvern, Hollybush, Birts Street and Welland.

Grog-tempered (GROG)

The texture of this sample, containing angular well-defined fragments of similar character to the groundmass, is typical of many Early to Middle Bronze Age vessels. Thin-sectioning of examples suggests that in some instances the fragments were denser, indurated pieces of the parent clay, indicating that there was little kneading of the clay before use and that it was used in a semi-plastic state. However, in this example, it is likely that the fragments have been fired before being added to the potting clay, removing the limestone inclusions and in some cases lowering the carbon content of the clay. These can indeed be classed as 'grog' although there is no conclusive evidence that the fragments are crushed fragments of broken pots, which is the current potting definition of the term.

The rounded quartz grains indicate that the clay originated somewhere in the Severn Valley and this suggests that the limestone inclusions are of Rhaetic or Jurassic limestone rather than Palaeozoic limestone, a major Iron Age fabric group in this part of the Severn Valley (Peacock 1968). The limestone was probably a bioclastic limestone in which the shell fragments were partially replaced by micrite. This is a very similar description to the limestone found in Peacock's Group B1, which he suggests is tempered with Palaeozoic limestone. However, there are not enough distinctive fragments present in the thin-section to confirm this identification, and the presence of an echinoid shell fragment does suggest the possibility of a Jurassic origin, perhaps in the Inferior Oolite which caps Bredon Hill, 8km to the north of this site.

Forms and decoration
Most featured sherds (rims and decorated pieces) among the Bronze Age group are illustrated (Fig. 14, nos 1–9). Pieces not illustrated include examples of a detached thumbed strip from Ditch 1 and a fingernail-impressed sherd from Ditch 2. Identifiable forms occur primarily in fabric MALV and comprise jar-like vessels with simple, flattened (nos 1, 5, 7) or out-curved rims (no. 2) and bowls with distinctive T-shaped rims (nos 3–4).

None of the recovered rim sherds from jar-like vessels in fabric MALV were sufficient to reconstruct their original diameter. Such vessels are representative of plain bucket-urn type vessels, a more complete example of which was recorded in a similar fabric 1.2km further west at The Gastons (Timby 2004a, fig. 16, no. 2). Vessel no. 2 possibly represents a globular urn. This vessel together with two further examples (nos 3 and 4) feature applied strip decoration. Other instances of decoration consist of fingertip or fingernail impressions and one instance of scoring (no. 7). One of the T-shaped rimmed bowls features finger-tip decoration on its external projection.

Identifiable forms among the non-Malvernian fabrics present are restricted to rim sherds from jar-like vessels exhibiting barrel-shaped or ovoid and globular profiles (no. 8). Both forms could be accommodated within the barrel or globular urn series which characterise some Middle Bronze Age assemblages. The small grog-tempered group comprised undecorated bodysherds. These are thick-walled, in the range 10–16mm, comparable to the other fabrics represented.

Stylistic affinities and dating
Radiocarbon determinations were obtained from burnt food residues preserved on sherds in Malvernian fabric MALV from Ditch 1 (Table 14). Dates of 1530–1410 cal. BC for a sherd from fill 5366 and 1440–1290 cal. BC for a T-shaped rimmed bowl (Fig. 14, no. 4), determined at 95.4% confidence, confirm the Middle Bronze Age dating. The majority of identifiable forms and the radiocarbon determinations relate to Ditch 1 and consequently there is no good evidence from the pottery to indicate that the use of Ditch 2 was closely contemporaneous. An indication that this may not be the case is the differences in fabric representation between the two features, in particular the presence of fabric SH in Ditch 2 and its absence from Ditch 1.

Characteristics of form/decoration present primarily in the pottery from Ditch 1 include bucket urn vessels and the use of applied strips, which show affinities with the primarily southern English Deverel Rimbury style. The distinctive bowl forms (Fig. 14, nos 3–4; Timby 2004a, fig. 16, no. 3) and use of impressed fingernail decoration (Fig. 14, no. 5), are absent from the southern English corpus and hint at a regional sub-style. Further evidence for this comes from the mainly funerary group from Bevan's Quarry, Temple Guiting. This site 20km to the south-east of Tewkesbury included a bowl of similar type (O'Neil 1967, fig. 3, no. 2a) and instances of impressed fingernail decoration. The latter was also recorded on a vessel from Birdlip (Woodward 1998, fig. 26, no. 3) and may be representative of the survival of an Early Bronze Age decorative tradition.

Vessel nos 3–4, and a possible third recovered from Ditch 1 in the evaluation (Timby 2004a, fig. 16, no. 3), find their closest parallels among the so-called 'cauldron pots' from the Upper Thames Valley, for example Mount Farm, Dorchester, Oxfordshire (Myres 1937, fig. 7; Harding 1974, 3). The Early Iron Age dating of the Oxfordshire vessels is difficult to dispute from the evidence presented. This being the case, similarities are probably coincidental or more apparent than real. Certainly the lower profile of vessel no. 3 differs from the more rounded vessels from the Mount Farm series (Myres 1937, fig. 7).

Discussion (incorporating comments by Alan Vince)
Although recent publications have added to our knowledge of the Middle Bronze Age in the north Gloucestershire/Warwickshire/Worcestershire region (Timby 2003; Timby 2004a; Woodward 1998, 66–7) the corpus of later 2nd-millennium BC pottery remains small. The Rudgeway Lane group is significant, accompanied as it is by absolute dating and seemingly representing a regional expression of the tradition current in the Middle Bronze Age in southern England. The dating is consistent with that proposed on stylistic grounds (*c.* 1500–1150 BC) for the spear mould(s) recovered from Site F on the Eastern Relief Road (Needham 2004, 62–6), and confirms significant activity in this area in the Middle Bronze Age. Evidence for the use of the Malvernian vessels comprised burnt food residues on three vessels (including bowl no. 4 and 'urn' no. 1) and external sooting on three vessels. This evidence, together with the fragmented and dispersed character of the assemblage, is consistent with domestic usage.

Although differing in the geological origin of its coarse inclusions, the Malvernian fabric is reminiscent of the coarse flint-tempered fabrics which typify Middle Bronze Age 'Urn' assemblages from southern England. Exploitation of Malvernian clays or rock inclusions may have begun during the Middle Bronze Age, a date also supported by finds from Much Marcle, Herefordshire (T.C. Darvill, pers. comm.) and Kemerton, Worcestershire (A. Hancocks, pers. comm.). The samples subjected to petrographical analysis exhibited very similar composition to Peacock's (1968) and it is very likely that they are ancestral to the Iron Age ware. By contrast, they are rather different to the handmade Early Roman ware and the medieval 12th to 13th-century ware, both of which contain much less hornblend and no examples of dolerite or altered rhyolite. The industry therefore seems to have been moved a few miles to the north following the Roman conquest and then shifted further east in the medieval period. It is unlikely that the latter two industries have any connection with each other whereas it is quite possible that the shift from the area east of Midsummer Hill to the north took place over a relatively short period of time.

It would be nice to claim the grog-tempered ware as being similarly ancestral to Peacock's Group B1 limestone-tempered ware vessels. However, the presence of a fragment of echinoid shell in the Rudgeway Lane sample and no definite fragments of brachiopod shell, crinoids or bryozoan fragments, all of which occur in Peacock's Group B, argues against this. Nevertheless, this identification cannot be ruled out and further investigation, either through further thin-sectioning or chemical analysis, might be able to test the matter conclusively.

Period 2: Middle Iron Age (c. 4th to 2nd century BC)

Pottery amounting to 27 sherds (317g) is considered to date to this period on the basis of fabric or vessel form/decoration (Table 3). The small quantities of stratified material present derive from the fills of Enclosure 1. The bulk of this material consists of bodysherds in coarse fossil shell-tempered fabric. In the absence of indications of dating from vessel form, broadly Iron Age dating is suggested on the basis of similarities in the fabrics here and those from better-dated groups from the region (Hancocks 1999; McSloy 2006). Pottery of more certain Middle Iron Age date was present as a single sherd from Enclosure 1 (Fig. 14, no. 10) and as residual finds within Period 4 features (Fig. 14, nos 11–12). This material consists of sherds in Malvernian rock-tempered fabric, MAL A, distinguishable from Late Iron Age/Early Roman material in this fabric through the presence of impressed, or scored and impressed decoration. Decorated material of this type is characteristic of Malvernian assemblages dating to the c. 4th/3rd to 1st centuries BC (Peacock 1968). A vessel with a small loop-handle (Fig. 14, no. 12) is also consistent with a Middle Iron Age date, although such forms are more usually encountered in assemblages further to the east.

Table 3: Quantification of the Middle Iron Age pottery by sherd count (c), minimum number of vessels (mv) and weight (w; in grammes)

Fabric	Period 2 (Enc 1)	Period 3	Period 4	Total
	c/mv/w	c/mv/w	c/mv/w	c/mv/w
IA SH	1/1/114	10/7/44	10/8/74	**21/16/232**
MAL A	1/1/13	3/1/42	2/2/30	**6/4/85**
Totals	*2/2/127*	*13/8/86*	*12/10/104*	*27/20/317*

Fabric

IA SH
Handmade. Inclusions are moderately well sorted comprising common medium or coarse (in range 0.5–3mm) sub-angular yellowish limestone and common medium to coarse (in range 0.5–2mm) fossil shell and other fossiliferous material. Fabric is soft with a soapy feel and irregular or laminated fracture. Reddish-brown surfaces with dark grey core.

MAL A
As type MAL RE A 1 (*Late Iron Age to Early Roman, below*).

Catalogue of illustrated prehistoric sherds (Fig. 14)

Middle Bronze Age

1   Handmade probable bucket urn with flattened slightly expanded rim, fabric MALV. Fill of Ditch 1 (Area A), Period 1.
2   Handmade ?globular urn with out-curved rim and vertical, finger-impressed applied strip decoration, fabric MALV. Fill of Ditch 1 (Area A), Period 1.
3   Handmade large bowl with T-shaped rim and finger-tipping on outer rim edge, fabric MALV. Fill of Ditch 1 (Area A), Period 1.

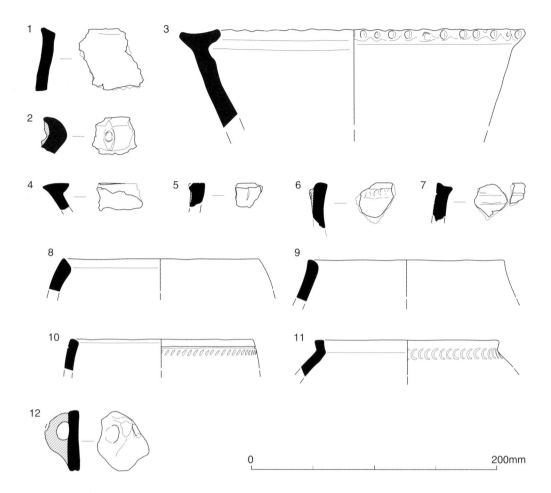

Fig. 14: Prehistoric pottery (scale 1:3)

4   Handmade T-shaped rim from bowl, fabric MALV. Fill of Ditch 1 (Area A), Period 1.
5   Handmade bucket/barrel urn with flattened, slightly expanded rim and fingernail impressions below
     rim, fabric MALV. Fill of Ditch 1 (Area A), Period 1.
6   Handmade sherd with horizontal impressed, applied strip decoration and coil break to upper body,
     fabric MALV. Fill of Ditch 6 (Area D), Period 3.
7   Handmade bucket/barrel urn with flattened, slightly expanded rim and ?scored decoration below rim,
     fabric MALV. Fill of Ditch 2 (Area A), Period 1.
8   Handmade barrel urn? (or ovoid vessel) with internal rim bevel, fabric SH. Fill of Ditch 2 (Area A),
     Period 1.
9   Handmade ?globular urn with simple, upright rim, fabric SH. Fill of Ditch 2 (Area A), Period 1.

Middle Iron Age
10   Handmade barrel-shaped jar with simple rim and impressed and scored decoration below rim, fabric
     MAL A. Fill of Ditch 6530 (part of Trackway 1 and Enclosure 4, Area D). Phase 4b.
11   Handmade rounded/globular jar with upright, squared rim and impressed crescent decoration below
     rim, fabric MAL A. Fill of Ditch 5880 (part of Enclosure 1, Area D). Period 2.
12   Handmade jar sherd with ?countersunk loop handle, fabric MAL A. Fill of Ditch 6530 (part of Trackway
     1 and Enclosure 4, Area D). Phase 4b.

The Late Iron Age and Roman pottery (1st to 4th century AD)

A total of 5838 sherds (81.9kg) of Late Iron Age and Roman pottery was recovered (Table 4). The large bulk of this material was of Roman date and derived from Area D. Methodologies adopted are comparable to those used on the Eastern Relief Road (Timby 2004b). The pottery was sorted into fabric types and quantified by sherd count, weight and estimated vessel equivalent (EVE) for each excavated context. The majority of the pottery, 77% by sherd count, was recovered from linear features, primarily those associated with the Period 4 enclosures; 9% was derived from pits or postholes; 6% from the well and the remainder from miscellaneous contexts. The average sherd weight of 14g was notably higher than that in the Eastern Relief Road assemblages at 10g and reflects of a number of substantially complete vessels recorded from contexts such as 7135 and 7044 associated with the well. In common with the assemblage from the neighbouring sites, surface preservation was generally poor, in some instances presenting difficulties in identification.

Assemblage composition

Fabrics
Coding of fabrics, unless otherwise indicated, is that utilised on the Eastern Relief Road (Timby 2004b). Reference is made to previously published descriptions, including the National Roman Fabric Reference Collection (Tomber and Dore 1998) and the Worcestershire pottery type series (Bryant and Evans 2004a). Roman pottery types are wheel-thrown unless otherwise stated.

Late Iron Age to Early Roman

Malvernian 'native type' igneous/metamorphic rock-tempered (MAL RE A 1)
Handmade Malvernian rock tempered ware (Peacock 1968, Group A; Tomber and Dore 1998, 147).
Forms: neckless jars of 'tubby cook pot' type (Fig. 15, nos 15–16); fewer Black-burnished ware 1 (BB1) derived everted-rim jars, bead or flat-rimmed dishes (Fig. 15, no. 24).
Dating: jars represent an Iron Age tradition which extended into the 2nd century AD (Peacock 1967; Evans et al. 2000, 44). Dating for BB1 derived forms probably reflects the mainly Antonine/early 3rd-century AD date of the forms copied.

Malvernian 'Native type' Palaeozoic limestone-tempered (MAL RE B)
Handmade Malvernian limestone-tempered ware. (Peacock 1968, Group B1).
Forms: rounded mid-sized jars with everted rims (Fig. 15, nos 13–4); fewer, large storage jars with bead or 'hammer-head' rims (MALL2 in Timby 2004b).
Dating: undecorated jars of the type represented here are typical of the Late Iron Age and continue into the early Roman (probably pre-Flavian) period. Storage jars may continue later.

'Belgic' grog-tempered (BGROG)
Wheel-thrown grog-tempered ware. Soft, grey fabric with common dark grey grog and occasional quartz. Possibly as Worcester fabric 8 (Bryant and Evans 2004a, 246). Fabrics/forms compare to 1st-century BC/AD 'Belgic'-type wares from south-east England (Thompson 1982). A post-Conquest date is usually assumed for the material from this region.
Forms: Necked bowls and jars with out-curved or bead rims (Fig. 15, no. 17). Raised cordon below neck.
Dating: mid-1st century AD.

'Belgic' sandy type (BQZ)
Wheel-thrown fine, black-firing fabric with grey core. Slightly micaceous. As Worcester fabric 7 (Bryant and Evans 2004a, 246).

Table 4: Quantification of the late Iron Age and Roman pottery by sherd count (c), weight (w; in grammes) and rim-estimated vessel equivalents (EVEs)

Period/Phase	3	4	4a	4b	4c	5	Unphased	Totals
Fabric	c/w/EVEs	c/w/EVEs	c/w/EVEs	c/w/EVEs	c/w/EVEs	c/w/EVEs	c/w/EVEs	c/w/EVEs
LGF SA	–	1/10/.07	–	3/25/.14	–	–	1/2/.03	5/37/.24
LMV SA	–	1/3/.04	–	3/19/.11	–	–	4/62/–	8/84/.15
LEZ SA	–	8/67/.05	–	42/287/.27	4/28/.05	–	–	54/380/.37
EG SA	–	–	–	2/13/.03	–	–	–	2/13/.03
CNG BS	–	–	–	1/4/–	–	–	–	1/4/–
SVW OX	43/570/.48	428/13541/5.03	25/408/.86	1695/26933/14.65	153/1936/1.89	26/75/–	217/2334/2.14	2587/45797/25.05
SVW char	1/61/–	2/113/–	5/166/–	41/771/–	–	–	23/398/.26	72/1509/.26
SVW mort	–	–	–	6/275/.47	–	–	–	6/275/.47
MAL RE A 1	286/1517/.20	22/190/.12	9/45/–	275/3310/1.87	28/424/.13	6/29/–	159/1139/.32	785/6654/2.64
MAL RE B	330/2257/.96	11/61/–	12/23/–	119/527/.23	5/18/–	7/31/–	165/593/.13	649/3500/1.32
MAL RE A 2	1/1/–	33/581/.92	–	227/3095/1.95	58/606/.43	1/2/–	29/290/.50	349/4575/3.80
MAL SLAB	3/139/–	55/2501/na.	1/12/–	153/7067/na.	32/516/na.	–	15/226/na	258/10449/na
BGROG	23/224/.21	3/39/–	–	16/70/–	–	2/12/–	2/19/.04	47/376/.25
BQZ	51/474/.48	–	–	–	–	–	–	51/474/.48
DOR BB1	4/22/.10	24/158/.23	–	469/3588/3.89	43/313/.27	11/10/	32/129/.36	583/4220/4.85
OXF RS	–	3/38/–	–	57/115/–	3/53/.08	2/2/–	1/3/–	66/211/.08
OXF WH	–	–	–	3/36/–	5/293/.25	–	–	8/329/.25
MAH WH	–	8/67/–	–	2/36/.04	–	–	–	10/103/.04
BB IM	–	–	–	8/145/–	9/417/.23	–	–	17/562/.23
SAV GT	–	–	–	2/43/–	–	–	–	2/43/–
ROM SH	–	–	–	3/38/–	1/12/–	1/1/–	–	5/51/–
GW fine	–	6/42/.04	–	60/468/.89	9/49/–	2/6/–	12/98/–	89/663/.93
GW coarse	–	2/12/–	1/7/–	37/341/.19	9/20/–	–	25/152/.08	74/532/.27
GW MIC	–	2/34/–	–	10/52/.17	14/113/.20	–	3/55/.15	29/254/.52
LOC GROG	–	–	–	16/191/–	1/6/–	–	–	17/197/–
CC misc	–	–	–	2/7/–	–	–	1/2/–	3/9/–
OXID	7/42/–	–	–	46/568/.38	3/9/–	–	1/12/–	57/631/.38
WHf	1/1/–	–	–	2/5/–	–	–	1/3/–	4/9/–
Totals	*743/5266/2.43*	*616/17499/6.5*	*53/661/.86*	*3300/48029/25.28*	*377/4813/3.53*	*58/168/–*	*691/5455/4.01*	*5838/81941/42.61*

Forms: Carinated bowl with multiple cordons and scored decoration.
Dating: mid/late 1st century AD.

Roman (local)

Severn Valley ware (SVW)

SVW OX: Severn Valley Ware (Tomber and Dore 1998, 149). Included is the reduced-firing variant (<1%) and the type containing fine igneous/metamorphic rock (3%) which suggests a Malvern source.

Forms (classified after Webster 1976): the assemblage is dominated by jars of medium and narrow-mouthed form (type A), which constitute 43%, and wide-mouthed, with flaring/triangular rim (type C) which provide 17.5%; also represented are tankards (type E) 16%; curved-sided bowls (type F) or platters/dishes (type K) 4%; and carinated cups/bowls (type H) 1%. Other forms, each under 1% by EVEs, include samian-derived bowls (type I), strainer bowls (Webster 1976, no. 58) and lids (type L). Of note is a costrel (Fig. 16, no. 40), a form previously unrecognised in this ware.

Dating: production occurred throughout Roman period. Early forms include carinated cups/bowls (Fig. 15, no. 19), platters (Fig. 15, no. 21) and a possible butt-beaker copy (Fig. 15, no. 20). Most of the forms, such as tankards (Fig. 15, nos. 25/28) and wide-mouthed jars and bowls (Fig. 15, no. 27) date broadly to the 2nd/3rd century (Webster 1976; Evans *et al.* 2000). 'Pulley-rim' jars (Fig. 15, no. 30) and flaring tankards are probably 3rd or 4th century in date.

SVW char: Severn Valley Ware variant characterised by charcoal/other organic inclusions. As Worcester fabric 12.2 (Bryant and Evans 2004a, 250–3).
Forms: medium-mouthed jars (type A); tankards (type E), and carinated bowls (type H).
Dating: more commonly earlier Roman (1st and 2nd centuries).

SVW mort: Severn Valley Ware mortaria fabric. As Worcester fabric 37 (Bryant and Evans 2004a, 257).
Forms: mortarium with bead and angular flange (Fig. 15, no. 26).
Dating: 1st to earlier 2nd centuries.

Malvernian grey (MAL RE A 2)

Wheel-thrown or handmade. A distinction is made here between native-type and 'Romanised' Malvernian wares (as with the Eastern Relief Road sites; Timby 2004b). Vessels are typically reduced to mid-grey, are mostly wheel-thrown and occur mostly as Black-burnished ware derived jar and other forms (below).
Forms: large jars with flaring everted rims; flat-rimmed and flanged bowls; plain-rimmed dishes; knobbed lids.
Dating: probably mainly 3rd to 4th centuries.

Malvernian slab-built (MAL SLAB)

Handmade. Classified as 'ceramic circular tiles' on the Relief Road sites, where only the flat, rounded elements occurred. The fabric is a coarser version of MAL RE A with abundant large igneous/metamorphic rock inclusions. Comparable material occurs at Droitwich (Hurst and Woodiwiss 1992, fig. 46, no. 3) and Worcester, where possible functions are discussed (Bryant and Evans 2004b, 366–7). The most likely use is as a form of press, for the processing/preservation of meat or cheese. Wall-perforations noted on vessel no. 36 may lend further weight to this interpretation.
Forms: Consist of two separate elements: Thick-walled, open (?baseless) vessel with applied ledge supports and circular perforations (Fig. 16, no. 36a/b) and sub-rectangular plates (Fig. 16, no. 37).
Dating: later Roman dating (3rd to 4th centuries) is most often applied (Bryant and Evans 2004b, 366). This date is reinforced here as the material is most abundant in Phase 4c.

Roman (regional)

Dorset Black-burnished ware (DOR BB1)

Handmade. Dorset Black-Burnished ware (Tomber and Dore 1998, 127). From Poole Harbour region, Dorset.
Forms: the range of forms is comparable to the Eastern Relief Road assemblage. Calculated by rim EVE the assemblage comprises everted-rim jars/cooking pots (Holbrook and Bidwell 1991, 95–6) 64%; bead-rim dishes (ibid., 96) 1%; plain-rimmed dishes (ibid., 99–100) 24%; flat-rimmed bowls/dishes (ibid., 97–8) 8%; flat grooved-rim dishes/bowls (ibid., 98); 4% conical flanged bowls (ibid., 98–9) 2%.

Dating: the ware is unlikely to appear at this site before *c.* AD 120. The forms predominantly date to the 2nd or earlier 3rd century (see phase 4b/c discussion). The few late forms (after *c.* AD 250) include jars with obtuse-angled lattice decoration and flanged bowls.

Oxfordshire red-slipped ware (OXF RS)
Oxfordshire red/brown colour-coated ware (Tomber and Dore 1998, 176).
Forms: bowl sherd of uncertain type; flanged mortarium of Young type C100 (Young 1977, 174).
Dating: in production *c.* AD 240. Probably not widespread until after *c.* AD 270/300. Mortarium C100 is a 4th-century form.

Oxfordshire whitewares (OXF WH)
Oxfordshire whiteware including mortaria (Tomber and Dore 1998, 175).
Forms: flanged mortaria of Young type M22 (Young 1977, 76).
Dating: in production from the 2nd century AD. M22 mortaria date from *c.* AD 240 and are commonest after *c.* AD 300.

Midlands mortaria (MAH WH)
Mancetter-Hartshill mortaria (Tomber and Dore 1998, 189).
Forms: one example of a curved-flange mortarium.
Dating: in production from the 2nd century AD.

Savernake wares (SAV GT)
Savernake grog-tempered ware (Tomber and Dore 1998, 191).
Forms: bodysherds only.
Dating: 1st and earlier 2nd century AD.

Roman shell-tempered (ROM SH)
Most of the material represented is visibly coarser than Harrold shell-tempered ware (Tomber and Dore 1998, 115) and is comparable to material from Wormington, Gloucestershire, which possibly has an Oxfordshire source (McSloy 2006, 39).
Forms: bodysherds only.
Dating: uncertain, but occurs in Phases 4b/4c.

Late imitation Black-burnished ware (BB IM)
Vessels imitating Dorset Black-Burnished ware forms in a coarse, dark-firing reduced fabric. Similar material (TF 206) occurs in 4th-century AD deposits in Gloucester (Ireland 1983, 101) and Cirencester (fabrics 118/119; Keely 1986, 161–2).
Forms: conical flanged bowl, plain-rimmed dish (Fig. 16, nos 33–4).

Roman (continental)

Samian (Samian)
LGF SA: South Gaulish (La Graufesenque).
LMV SA: Central Gaulish (Les Martres-de-Veyre).
LEZ SA: Central Gaulish (Lezoux) samian.
EG SA: East Gaulish samian.

Central Gaulish black-slipped ware (CNG BS)
Occurs as a single beaker sherd (Tomber and Dore 1998, 50).

Roman (Unclassified)

The following fabrics occur in modest quantities and are of uncertain source. Similarity to material from among larger published assemblages in the region suggests fairly local manufacture in most instances.

GW fine: inclusionless or slightly sandy, typically mid-grey throughout. Occasional use of clay rustication. As Worcester fabric 14 (Bryant and Evans 2004a, 257).

GW coarse: sandy reduced ware, typically dark grey firing. As Worcester fabric 15 (Bryant and Evans 2004a, 259–60).

GW MIC: coarse, micaceous greyware. As Gloucester fabric TF5 (Ireland 1983, 99).

LOC GROG: ?handmade grey-firing grogged fabric. As Worcester fabric 16 (Bryant and Evans 2004a, 259).

CC misc: fine oxidised fabric with orange-brown colour-coat. As Worcester fabric 31 (Bryant and Evans 2004a, 263).

OXID: miscellaneous sandy oxidised wares. As Worcester fabric 13 (Bryant and Evans 2004a, 257).

WHf: miscellaneous sandy whiteware. Possibly Oxfordshire products.

Description by period

Period 3: c. 1st century AD

The Period 3 assemblage is dominated by handmade 'native' wares, types originating from the Malverns and spanning the Late Iron Age and Early Roman periods. The presence of Severn Valley wares and the 'Belgic' types, which occur in small quantities throughout, implies that at least part of this assemblage dates to the 1st century AD and most probably the middle decades of this century.

The pottery was principally recovered from Ditches 3/4 and Enclosure 3. Average sherd weight (6.5g) is lower than for subsequent periods and is reflective of a fairly heavily fragmented group. Malvernian fabrics (MAL RE B and MAL RE A 1) in Iron Age traditions represent 83% (by sherd count) of the Period total (Table 4). 'Belgic' types (BGROG and BQZ), together with quantities of Severn Valley ware, indicate that a proportion at least of the assemblage dates to the period following c. AD 50, and conceivably to the later years of the 1st century AD.

Forms amongst the Malvernian limestone-tempered wares (MAL RE B) comprise mainly mid-sized jars with rounded profiles and everted-rims (Fig. 15, nos 13–14) which are familiar from sites in the region and exported beyond (Timby and Harrison 2004). A small number of large storage jars with heavy 'hammer-head' rims (Spencer 1983, 415, fig. 3) are also present. Forms among the rock-tempered group consist of mid-sized jars exhibiting straight-sided or slack-shouldered profiles (Fig. 15, no. 15). Exterior sooting on these native-type vessels suggests use as cooking vessels.

Forms among the wheel-thrown grog-tempered (BGROG) and related wares (BQZ) consist of necked/cordoned (Fig. 15, no. 17) and carinated/cordoned (Fig. 15, no. 18) bowl forms. Similarly, the Severn Valley ware forms are predominantly non-utilitarian, mostly Webster (1976) type H carinated cups/bowls and straight-sided tankards. Samian and other continental finewares are absent from Period 3 and it is conceivable that the sherd of Flavian samian found residually in later phases might have reached the site in this period.

Quantities of pottery (68 sherds weighing 338g) comprising Malvernian limestone and rock-tempered types and Droitwich briquetage (101g) were recovered from evaluation trench 8. Later Iron Age/ Early Roman dating corresponding to that of the larger Period 3 excavation assemblage is likely for this material.

Phase 4a: 1st to 2nd century AD

Only small quantities of pottery were recovered from features assigned to this phase. The range of fabrics represented is restricted and similar to Period 3, although significantly Severn Valley ware is now the dominant type. Only a few identifiable forms are present including a near complete platter (Fig. 15, no. 21), which is closer to its Gallo-Belgic progenitors than the devolved forms illustrated by Webster (1976, 36, fig. 10, nos 69–71).

Phase 4b: 2nd to late 3rd or early 4th century AD

Pottery from this, the most intense phase of Roman activity, amounted to 3318 sherds (23.93 EVEs) or 76% of the Period 4 assemblage. Whilst the pottery suggests a relatively broad dating there is an emphasis on the period from the 2nd to early/mid 3rd century in the larger discrete groups recovered from the enclosure ditches and internal features (Table 5).

The groups are dominated by Severn Valley wares (61% of total EVEs), occurring primarily as jars, wide-mouthed bowls and tankards (Fig. 15, nos 25 and 28). Malvernian igneous/metamorphic types including native (MAL RE A 1); 'Romanised' (MAL RE A 2) and 'slab-built' (MAL SLAB) varieties are well-represented (20% by count). There are roughly equal proportions of 'native' MAL RE A and the wheelthrown MAL RE A 2

Table 5: *Quantification of Phase 4b/4c pottery groups by sherd count, weight in grammes and rim-estimated vessel equivalents (EVEs)*

	Phase 4b 'early'					
Fabric Group	*North track* 6125	*Enc. 4* 6249	*Enc. 4* 6432	*Enc. 11/12* 6542	*Pit: 660* Pit Group 21	***Totals***
Samian	1/2/–	3/15/.03	2/15/.02	3/15/.03	2/28/–	*11/75/.08*
SVW	27/433/.20	55/303/.18	14/481/.75	31/727/.52	40/1095/1.08	*167/3039/2.73*
MAL RE A 2	–	–	12/40/–	6/99/.03	–	*18/139/.03*
MAL SLAB	–	–	–	–	2/234/–	*2/234/–*
MAL RE A 1	23/402/–	2/8/–	5/122/.20	3/109/–	18/303/.31	*51/944/0.51*
DOR BB1	4/23/.04	30/144/.23	9/68/.10	23/172/.18	5/22/–	*71/429/.55*
MAH WH	–	–	–	1/7/–	–	*1/7/–*
Misc.	–	4/14/.10	1/27/–	1/10/–	1/3/–	*7/54/.10*
Totals	***55/860/.24***	***94:476/.54***	***43/753/1.05***	***68/1139/.76***	***68/1685/1.39***	***328/4913/3.98***

	Phase 4b 'late'			Phase 4b/4c		
Fabric Group	*Enc. 4* 5908	*Enc. 11/12* 6796	*Ring Ditch 2* 6553	*Enc. 12* 5930	*Enc. 4* 6545	***Totals***
Samian	–	–	–	2/55/.04	3/28/.05	*5/83/.09*
SVW	74/1143/.33	11/163/.50	15/174/.23/1.06	77/1694/1.20	44/651/.60	*221/3825/3.69*
MAL RE A 2	28/400/.36	8/133/–	10/93/–	15/255/.55	33/337/.25	*94/1218/1.16*
MAL SLAB	–	2/166/–	1/295/–	13/252/–	5/380/–	*21/1093/–*
MAL RE A 1	7/118/.11	–	9/114/.08	3/50/–	3/33/–	*24/315/.19*
DOR BB1	11/109/.28	39/49/.20	11/86/.23	5/48/–	25/226/.14	*91/518/.85*
OXF RS	1/19/–	–	–	1/18/–	2/21/–	*4/58/–*
OXF WH	–	1/28/–	–	–	3/169/.25	*4/197/.25*
MAH WH	–	–	–	7/58/–	–	*7/58/–*
ROM SH	3/4/–	–	–	–	1/62/–	*4/66/–*
Misc.	19/223/–	2/7/–	7/49/–	1/3/–	5/302/.18	*34/584/.18*
Totals	***143/2016/1.08***	***63/546/.70***	***53/811/1.37***	***124/2430/1.79***	***123/2209/1.47***	***506/8012/6.41***

varieties, although it seems clear from the selected groups that the wheelthrown fabric is in the ascendant in later groups (Table 5). The absence of limestone-tempered Malvernian ware from these groups is also significant, suggesting that such material is wholly residual by the 2nd century. Forms in Malvernian wares, primarily MAL RE A, comprise 'tubby cooking pot' type jars with fewer Black-burnished ware derived forms.

Regional coarsewares represent 16% (by EVEs), the bulk of this material consisting of Dorset Black-burnished ware (DOR BB1) which occurs as everted-rim jars, dishes and bowls, common to 'exported' groups in this ware (Table 4). Flaring-rim jars with obtuse-angled lattice decoration and conical flanged bowls are present in 'late' Phase 4b groups, as are derived versions in imitative fabric BB IM. Mortaria primarily come from Midlands and Oxfordshire sources, although samian mortaria also occur.

Finewares and flagons are uncommon in the Period 4 assemblage. Scraps of colour-coated wares and white-slipped flagon fabrics similar to types known from Worcester or Gloucester are likely to derive from fairly local sources. Oxfordshire colour-coated bowls of uncertain type are present in 'later' groups. Most abundant are continental imports, principally Central Gaulish undecorated samian forms and one sherd from a Central Gaulish black-slipped ware beaker. The samian, whilst never common, is present routinely in the larger 'early' groups and notably absent in later ones (Table 5).

Phase 4c: late 3rd to 4th century AD
Relatively little pottery derived from Phase 4c deposits, sizeable groups being restricted to ditch 6504. Observable differences between Phases 4b/4c are slight, probably due to incorporation of residual material in the later groups. The quantities of Severn Valley Ware are reduced in Phase 4c compared to the previous phase and a charcoal-tempered variant (SVW char) is entirely absent. Malvernian fabrics, excluding native types (MAL RE A 1/B and MAL SLAB) are proportionally more common in the later phase (27% combined by count), as is Black-burnished 'imitation' fabric BB IM.

The well
Dating for the final sealing of this feature is provided by small quantities of pottery including material no earlier than the 3rd century AD (Fig. 16, no. 32). The bulk of material, including some substantially complete vessels (Fig. 16, nos 38–40), was recovered from primary silt 7144 and overlying layer 7135. A minimum of six Severn Valley ware vessels were present comprising narrow-mouthed jars and, more unusually, a costrel (Fig. 16, no. 40). The jar forms present and their largely complete state suggest these were losses in use, although deliberate structured deposition cannot be ruled out. The costrel, assuming use as a container for liquids, might also represent an accidental loss, although its rareness could be taken as another indication of a special deposit.

The costrel is previously unknown in Severn Valley ware, although similar forms occur exclusively in oxidised fabrics. The configuration of the present example is representative of the class as a whole: a fully closed body which is rilled at the top and base, a loop handle at the top and twin pre-firing perforations of unequal size. The vessel profile is bi-conical rather than the more usual barrel-shaped. Costrels of this form are not widely known (or published) from Britain, although their distribution suggests that they were minor products of various regional industries across southern Britain. A continental ancestry would seem likely and parallels are known from the Danube provinces (V. Swan, pers. comm.). Occurrence of the form among Legionary type wares at Caerleon (Boon 1966, fig. 2, no. 5), suggests use from the Early Roman period, a date supported by other examples in other fabrics. Findspots include Cambridge (Liversidge 1977), London (pers. comm. Rupert Featherby); Milton Keynes (Marney 1989, fig. 42, no. 25), and Wortley villa, Gloucestershire. The latter is displayed in Stroud Museum (Acc. No. WV93.220) and occurs in a white fabric, with banded red-painted decoration, which is identified as Oxfordshire parchment ware and may indicate continuance of the form into the Late Roman period.

Samian by P.V. Webster

Moderate quantities of South Gaulish samian of 1st/early 2nd-century date were present in Period 4b and later deposits, where it is most likely to be redeposited. No samian was stratified in Period 3 or Phase 4a contexts (Table 4). Some material from Les Martres-de-Veyre (*fl.* AD 100–120) was present, but most of the samian was from the Central Gaulish (Lezoux) centre and thus predominantly *c.* AD 120–200.

Represented forms demonstrate a preponderance of common plain forms (Table 6). Of the 12 forms listed, only form 37 is mould decorated. Of the 58 vessels present only 14 (24%) are cups, the remainder being bowls or dishes. What this means in terms of function is hard to ascertain. With the exception of the mortarium form 45, all could be tableware but, if so, the comparatively low percentage of cups suggests that drinking vessels in other materials were also used.

Table 6: Quantification of the Samian ware by vessel form and source

Form/Fabric	LGF SA	LMV SA	LEZ SA	EG SA	Total	%
18/31	–	1	4	–	5	8.62
18/31R	2	–		–	2	3.45
18/31 or 31	–	–	1	–	1	1.72
18/31R or 31R	–	–	1	–	1	1.72
27	1	–		–	1	1.72
31	–	–	11	–	11	18.97
31R	–	–	2	–	2	3.45
33	–	1	10	–	11	18.97
36	–	–	1	1	2	3.45
37	–	1	3	1	5	8.62
42	–	1	–	–	1	1.72
45	–	–	2	–	2	3.45
79	–	–	2	–	2	3.45
80	–	–	1	–	1	1.72
Bowl	1	2	7	–	10	17.24
Cup	–	–	1	–	1	1.72
Total	**4**	**6**	**46**	**2**	**58**	99.99
%	6.90	10.34	79.31	3.45	100.00	

Stamped and decorated samian

Form 33, Central Gaulish (LEZ SA). A basal sherd shows part of the stamp]CIANI. The complete stamp probably read ALBUCIANI and is attributed to Albucius of Lezoux; cf. Dickinson 1986, 186, no. 3.8 for a similar but slightly larger example. The adjectival ending to the stamp presumably implies production by an *officina* rather than by a single producer. c. AD 160–200. The easternmost ditch of Enclosures 7 and 8.

Form 37, Les Martres-de-Veyre (LMV SA). A body sherd shows panel decoration divided by bead rows above the edge of a basal wreath. The only extant panel shows the lower halves of two small gladiators, both apparently facing to the left (Oswald 1936–7, nos 1010 and 1027). A vessel with the same arrangement (and indeed possibly from the same mould) is illustrated by Terrisse (1968, pl.1, 107) among the work of Drusus I. c. AD 100–120. The easternmost ditch of Enclosure 4.

Discussion

The pottery assemblage suggests continuous activity in Area D between the 1st and 4th centuries AD. The large bulk of it derives from the enclosures and other features associated with Phase 4b, whilst the Phase 4c assemblage is much smaller and consistent with contraction and abandonment during the 4th century. That assemblage highlights the difficulties of dating later Roman material in the absence of large ceramic groups or coin evidence.

The pattern of supply apparent within the Period 4 pottery is comparable with previously published assemblages from the Tewkesbury area (MacRobert 1993; Timby 2004b). Severn Valley wares are dominant (57% by weight), with Malvernian wares and Dorset Black-burnished ware accounting for the bulk of the remainder (21% and 11% respectively). The consistency of these assemblages is (unsurprisingly) suggestive of a common pattern of supply, largely from local sources and hints at a similar chronological range. More exacting chronological comparisons and assessments of relative economic or functional aspects are hindered by the inherently conservative nature of the coarsewares. The scarcity of mould-decorated pieces among the samian is a feature shared with the Eastern Relief Road assemblage (Timby 2004b), though not with that from the 'small town' excavations (MacRobert 1993) and presumably reflects the lower economic status of the farmsteads. The low incidence of samian overall at this site (1.2% by count) is typical of 'lower-end' rural assemblages (Willis 1998).

With the exception of the costrel the range of forms is typical for rural sites. Jars, of all types, are dominant (61% by EVEs), with open forms (23%) and tankards (10%) accounting for the bulk of the remainder. A range of kitchen/storage and dairy-related tasks is indicated from the forms: evidence for collection and storage of water is implied from the well group (Fig. 16, nos 38–40), and from sherds of six vessels preserving white limey residues. Carbonised residues indicative of cooking are absent from the group but this is most probably the result of poor surface survival. The scarcity of flagons and beakers/cups (each constitutes less than 1%) and the total absence of amphorae highlight the utilitarian character of the assemblage and suggest that the adoption of Roman traditions of food preparation, eating and drinking was limited.

Catalogue of illustrated Late Iron Age and Roman sherds (Figs 15 and 16)

13 Handmade rounded jar with everted rim, fabric MAL RE B. Fill of Enclosure 3, Period 3.
14 Handmade rounded jar with everted rim, fabric MAL RE B. Fill of Ditch 4, Period 3.
15 Handmade straight-sided/slack-shouldered jar with plain rim, fabric MAL RE A 1. Fill of Enclosure 3, Period 3.

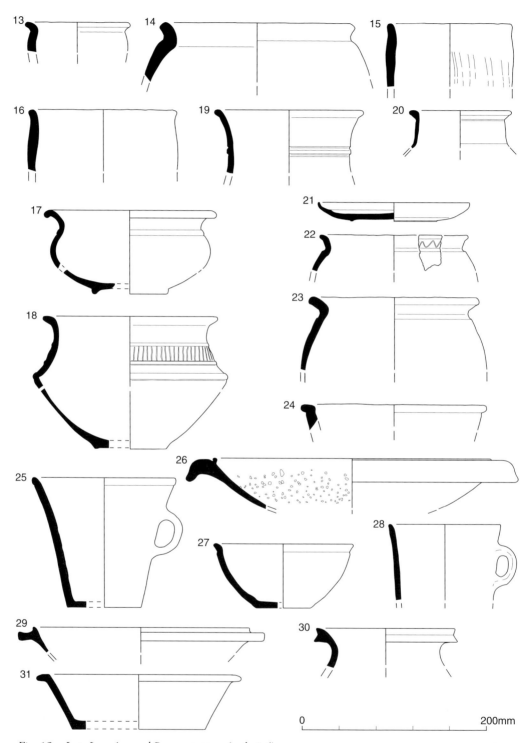

Fig. 15:   Late Iron Age and Roman pottery (scale 1:4)

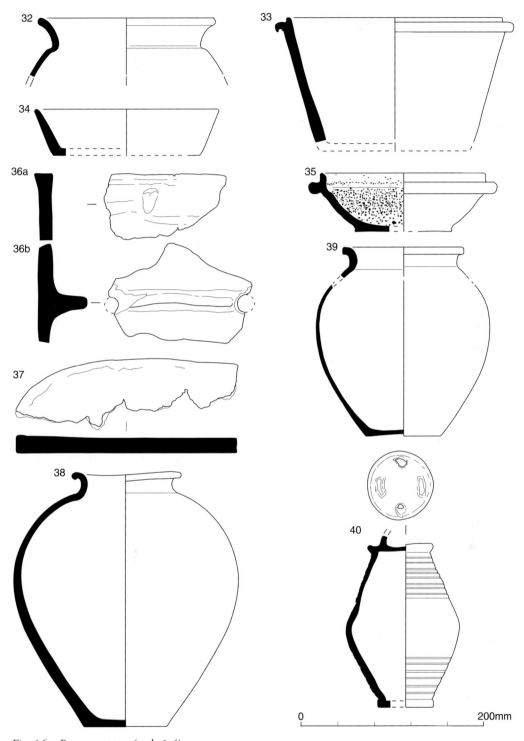

Fig. 16:   Roman pottery (scale 1:4)

16   Handmade straight-sided/slack-shouldered jar with plain rim, fabric MAL RE A 1. Fill of Enclosure 3, Phase 4a.

17   Wheel-thrown necked bowl with out-curved rim and cordon at neck, fabric BGROG. Fill of Enclosure 3, Period 3.

18   Wheel-thrown, carinated bowl with out-curved/triangular rim and multiple cordons and scored decoration, fabric BQZ. Fill of Enclosure 3, Period 3.

19   Wheel-thrown carinated bowl/cup (Webster 'H') with cordon at girth, fabric SVW OX. Fill of ditch 7068, Period 3.

20   Wheel-thrown beaker (Butt-Beaker derived), fabric SVW OX. Ditch fill of Enclosure 10, Phase 4b.

21   Wheel-thrown platter (Webster K), fabric SVW OX. Fill of ditch 6995 (internal to Enclosure 8), Phase 4a.

22   Handmade everted-rim jar with burnished wavy line at rim, fabric DOR BB1. Fill of northern trackway ditch, Phase 4b.

23   Wheel-thrown everted-rim jar (BB1 derived), fabric MAL RE A 2. Fill of pit 6660 part of Pit Group 21, Phase 4b.

24   Handmade? flat-rim dish or bowl (BB1 derived), fabric MAL RE A 1. Fill of pit 6660 part of Pit Group 21, Phase 4b.

25   Wheel-thrown tankard (Webster E), fabric SVW OX. Fill of Enclosure 9, gully 6496, Phase 4b.

26   Wheel-thrown mortarium with bead and curved flange, fabric SVW mort. Fill of northern trackway ditch, Phase 4b.

27   Wheel-thrown small, curved-sided bowl with short everted rim (Webster D), fabric SVW OX. Fill of Ditch 3, Period 3.

28   Wheel-thrown tankard (Webster H), fabric SVW OX. Ditch fill of Enclosure 4, Phase 4b.

29   Wheel-thrown bowl with flanged rim, fabric SVW OX. Ditch fill of Enclosure 11/12, Phase 4b.

30   Wheel-thrown necked jar with bifid/'pulley' rim, fabric SVW OX. Fill of posthole 6533, Group 11, Phase 4b.

31   Wheel-thrown dish with flat-rim, fabric MAL RE A 2. Ditch fill of Enclosure 11/12, Phase 4b.

32   Wheel-thrown everted-rim jar (BB1 derived), fabric MAL RE A 2. Upper fill of Well, Phase 4.

33   Wheel-thrown conical flanged bowl, fabric BB IM. Ditch fill of Enclosure 4, Phase 4c.

34   Wheel-thrown plain-rimmed dish, fabric BB IM. Ditch fill of Enclosure 4, Phase 4c.

35   Wheel-thrown mortarium, flanged?, OXF WH. (Young M22). Ditch fill of Enclosure 4, Phase 4c.

36   Handmade Malvernian 'slab-built' vessel, fabric MAL SLAB. Fill of ditch 6821 (north of Enclosure 4), Phase 4b.

37   Handmade Malvernian 'slab built' sub-rectangular plate, fabric MAL SLAB. Fill of ditch 6821 (north of Enclosure 4), Phase 4b.

38   Wheel-thrown narrow-mouthed, necked jar, fabric SVW OX. Primary fill of Well, Phase 4b.

39   Wheel-thrown medium-mouthed, necked jar, fabric SVW OX. Primary fill of Well, Phase 4b.

40   Wheel-thrown costrel, fabric SVW OX. Primary fill of Well, Phase 4b.

Other finds

The catalogue presented below is selective, with details of fragmentary or unidentifiable items, iron nails and unworked stone reserved for the archive. Metal objects other than nails were examined in the conservation laboratory and their condition assessed. Following assessment, which included x-radiography of metalwork, selected objects were cleaned to clarify their form. With the exception of socketed object no. 7, iron items are extensively corroded, some are fragmented, and most have soil adhering. Copper-alloy items display better preservation with original surfaces surviving in most instances.

The majority of metal and other items was recovered from Period 3 and 4 ditch deposits. Objects which are dateable by form are indicative of activity in the 1st and 2nd century AD and of the Late Roman period after *c*. AD 250. A small quantity of Anglo-Saxon artefacts, including the grave goods from the Period 5 inhumations, is described separately at the end of this section.

Copper alloy

Seventeen objects of copper alloy were recovered, the majority from Period 4 features. Fragmentary, functionally non-specific or unidentifiable objects are not included in this catalogue.

Brooches

Two fragments of Aucissa-type brooches, which are likely to be of pre-Flavian date, were recovered. They are presumably residual in their Phase 4b contexts though they may represent survivals in use. Aucissa brooches, the name relating to the occurrence on the head on some examples of the maker's name, are a continental form which arrived in Britain with the army after AD 43. Some, particularly uninscribed and smaller examples, are probably British made.

Fragments no. 3 and (not illustrated) RA 159 derive from brooches of uncertain type. The form of no. 3 would be consistent with a Colchester-derivative brooch, most likely of Polden Hill form, common in western Britain between the later 1st and 2nd centuries AD. RA 159 consists of the spring and pin from a two-piece open-sprung brooch. The limited number of coils and the pin length may suggest use with a trumpet-headed form.

1   Aucissa-type brooch (Fig. 17, no. 1). Axial bar is iron, with copper-alloy terminals. The head is uninscribed, but features a single knurled band at the junction with the bow. The bow is strongly ribbed and plain; the foot knob is plain. There are faint traces of cross grooves at the base of the bow. Length 57mm. Fill of northern trackway ditch, Phase 4b.

2   Fragments from a small Aucissa brooch (Fig. 17, no. 2). Strip-like bow with central channel and (probably) narrower flanking channels. The head is indistinct but probably uninscribed and undecorated. The foot knob is plain and pin missing. Length 36mm. Fill of ditch of Enclosure 5/6, Phase 4b.

3   Brooch fragment with traces of white-metal plating (Fig.17, no. 3). Lower part of bow with D-shaped section with narrow transverse rib. Cast, double-moulded foot knob and broad, unpierced catchplate. Surviving length 39mm. Fill of northern trackway ditch, Phase 4b.

n.i.   Pin from two-piece, sprung brooch with four coils to spring. Length 39mm. RA 159, fill of ditch of Enclosure 4, Phase 4b.

Bracelets

The fragmentary snake's head pennanular bracelet no. 5 is broadly dateable to between the 2nd and earlier 4th centuries AD (Johns 1996, 109–11). A similar and complete bracelet was recovered from an inhumation of 2nd-century AD date from Hucclecote, near Gloucester (Crummy 2003, 45). Broadly equivalent dating is likely for no. 4. The closest parallels, sharing characteristics of pennanular form and decorated, expanded terminals, are examples from Bancroft, Buckinghamshire (Hylton and Zeepvat 1994, fig. 140, nos 67–8). The remaining bracelets are of strip (no. 6) and cable (n.i.) type. Both are typical for the Late Roman period (after c. AD 250/70) with a 4th-century date likely for no. 6.

4   Fragmentary pennanular bracelet (Fig.17, no. 4). Expanded terminal with side notches and D-shaped section. Width at break 4mm; thickness at break 2.5mm. Fill of Ring Ditch 2, Phase 4b.

5   Fragmentary and distorted snake's head-terminal pennanular bracelet (Fig. 17, no. 5). cf. Johns' form Bii (Johns 1996, 109–11). D-shaped in section. Surviving length 31mm. Fill of ditch of Enclosure 4, Phase 4b.

6   Fragmentary strip bracelet with regular notches to outside edge (Fig. 17, no. 6). Tapered end from (soldered) join. Width 2mm; thickness 1mm. Fill of ditch of Enclosure 4, Phase 4c.

n.i.   Short length from a single strand, twisted bracelet. Width 2mm; thickness 1mm. RA 64. Fill of drying oven, Phase 4b.

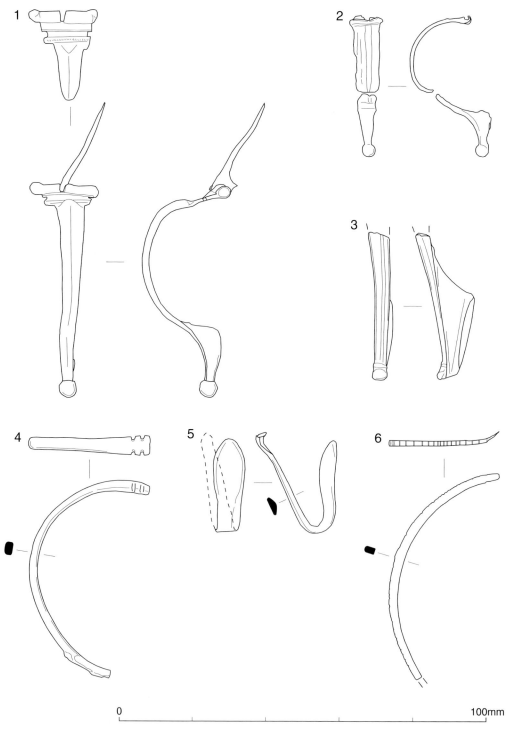

Fig. 17: Roman brooches nos 1–3 and bracelets nos 4–6 (scale 1:1)

Iron

A total of 89 iron items was recovered, primarily from Period 4 contexts. Functionally instructive objects, other than nails, are described below. Unidentifiable and/or fragmentary items, 'binding strips' and 49 nails are described only in the archive.

The function of socketed object no. 7 remains uncertain. The form of this object is close to that of a modern boat hook and to medieval objects ascribed this function (Goodall 1980, fig. 121, no. 170). A number of published parallels are known from Roman contexts, with differing functions proposed including weaponry/hunting implements (Gobel 1985, fig. 48, no. 1; Hylton 1996, 121) and thatching tools (Scott 1999, fig. 7.29, no. 596). The recovery of no. 7 from a well may imply an adapted use for the retrieval of lost buckets or other items.

7   Iron socketed implement with single barb with damage to socket and barb (Fig. 18). Round in section at the (split) socket, tapering to rectangular section close to tip. Surviving length 179mm. Fill 7144 of Well, Phase 4b.

n.i.   Socketed knife (Manning type 22). The blade, which is largely absent, is straight and is level with the upper line of the socket. The x-ray shows an elongated V-shaped split to the socket side. Surviving length 173mm; blade width (max.) 42mm. RA 165. Fill of ditch of Enclosure 4, Phase 4b.

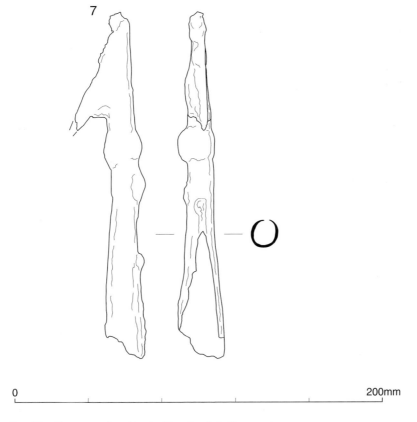

7

0   200mm

Fig. 18: Roman socketed iron object (scale 1:2)

n.i.   Unstratified ?reaping hook. The blade is mostly absent; it curves away from the socket at right angles. The socket is fully closed with overlapping ends. A single fastening rivet is visible from the x-ray. A Roman date is assumed, though the socket is unusually well formed compared to published examples (Manning 1985, 53–5). Surviving length 86.5mm.

n.i.   Double-spiked loop (Manning 1985, 130). The ends of both arms are splayed outwards. Length 75mm; diameter of loop 25mm. RA 150. Fill of ditch of Enclosure 4, Phase 4b.

Worked bone

n.i.   Shaft fragment from bird long bone (?tibia) with a single round hole into the cavity. The item appears polished from use. Possible flute or whistle fragment. Surviving length 32mm. Fill of ditch 6400, Phase 4a/b.

n.i.   Shaft fragment from sheep metapodial with transverse perforation. ?Toggle fragment. Surviving length 69mm. Fill of natural hollow, unphased.

n.i.   Cow-sized tibia fragment roughly worked to a point and polished from use. Surviving length 177mm. Fill of Ditch 4, Phase 3.

n.i.   Bone discoloured to green through contact with copper alloy. A plano-convex disc with central perforation from a decorative boss from a plate brooch or similar. Diameter 13mm; thickness 3mm. Fill of ditch of Enclosure 4, Phase 4b.

Glass

n.i.   Melon bead, approx. one half complete. Blue glass paste. Diameter 19mm. Unstratified.

Anglo-Saxon artefacts (Fig. 19)

A glass-headed iron pin was recovered from Period 4 layer 5989, a deposit approximately 10m to the north of Anglo-Saxon Burials 8 and 9. Nothing comparable in Cool's (1990) corpus of Roman pins has been identified and the closest parallels are from pagan Anglo-Saxon cemeteries. An example from Dover Buckland, Kent (Evison 1987, fig. 61, no. 3), derived from a female grave attributed to *c*. AD 650–75. The possibility that no. 8 represents a disturbed grave find should be considered.

8   Broken iron shank with glass head. Square-sectioned. Globular head is of natural green glass. Pin. Surviving length 35mm. Layer 5989, Period 4.

Burial 9

A number of grave goods were associated with this burial. Their location within the grave is shown on Fig. 12. The polychrome beads of glass and amber, nos 14 and 16–17, belong to types previously recognised from Anglo-Saxon cemeteries. Guido's type 3a (nos 14 and 16) occur across southern England, East Anglia and the Midlands (Guido 1999, 32). No. 17 is representative of a type more typically Kentish in its distribution (ibid. 63–4, Guido type 8xiv). Both are types known from the manufacturing site at Rothulfuashem, near Leiden, Netherlands, in operation *c*. AD 600 (ibid.). At the Dover Buckland cemetery (Evison 1987), polychrome beads of equivalent type were commonest in graves dated AD 575–625. Dating from continental sites is in broad agreement (Brugmann 2004, 42–3). Monochrome 'terracotta'-coloured bead no. 15 belongs to Guido's sub-melon class, where a segmented effect is achieved using rough nicks (Guido 1999, 61). The distribution pattern for beads of 6th-century AD date is primarily East Anglian, with outliers occuring along the Warwickshire Avon Valley. The irregular form of the amber beads appears typical for the Anglo-Saxon period, as is shown by examples from local sites (Evison and Hill 1996; Ford 2000) and among larger groups from eastern England (Evison 1987). The Dover

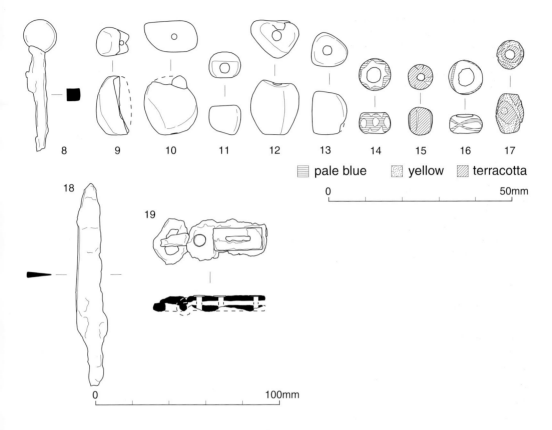

Fig. 19: Anglo-Saxon objects. Beads nos 8–17 (scale 1:1); iron knife and plate nos 18–19 (scale 1:2)

Buckland sample suggests that the number represented here was typical for a single grave. The main period of popularity of amber beads, based on the evidence from Buckland, was the 6th century (Evison 1987, 60).

The form of iron knife no. 18 is typical of knives presumed to be for personal use which are common finds from pagan Anglo-Saxon cemeteries including Beckford (Evison and Hill 1996, 21–2). Knives of broadly comparable form from Dover Buckland ('Type 1': Evison 1987, 113) occurred in all phases of the cemetery which was in use *c.* AD 475–750. Buckle set no. 19 shows affinities with examples from Anglo-Saxon cemeteries in the region including Beckford (Evison and Hill 1996, 21–2), and Bishop's Cleeve (Ford 2000, 85), and those in the Thames Valley (MacGregor and Bolick 1993, 191–208). The silvered copper-alloy embellishments are unusual.

9-13 Irregularly shaped amber beads perforated lengthways. No. 9 is fragmentary, broken post-deposition. Nos 10 and 12–13 range in length (12–15mm) and width (10–12mm). No. 11 is smaller: 8mm x 8mm.

14 Degraded opaque white-coloured glass bead, with blue crossed wave trail. 'Thick-annular' polychrome form. Evison type D24/Guido type 3a. Diameter 9mm.

15 Terracotta-coloured opaque glass over greenish translucent core. 'Sub-melon'/'nicked' barrel-shaped monochrome bead. Guido type 8vi. Length 9mm.

16   Degraded opaque white-coloured glass bead, with pale blue crossed wave trail. 'Thin annular' polychrome form. Evison type D26/Guido Guido type 3a. Diameter 9mm.

17   Opaque terracotta-coloured glass bead with yellow paste inlay, mostly missing. Barrel-shaped polychrome form. Evison type D46/Guido 8xiv(b). Length 10mm.

18   Iron knife with tang at centreline of blade. The blade back is straight, curving close to the tip. The cutting edge is damaged but appears to be straight. There are indications from the x-ray that the cutting edge (of ?steel) is welded on. Length 107mm.

19   D-shaped iron buckle and plate. The plate is formed from rectangular iron sheet, folded around the rear of the loop, with an internally slotted rectangular mount of silvered copper-alloy. The flattened head of a ?copper-alloy rivet immediately behind the loop is also silvered. Two further rivets are visible from the x-ray, in the positions indicated in the drawing. The rivet heads are not visible on the mount and it is unclear whether these were integral (cast as one with the mount) or sit behind it (which would necessitate the fixing of the mount by other means). Overall length 62mm.

Coins and tokens

Four Roman coins of copper alloy and a post-medieval lead token were recovered (Table 7). The poor condition of the Roman coins prevents full identification. The lead token belongs to a poorly understood class of artefact which most likely functioned as small change for use in taverns or similar (Hume 1969, 173).

Table 7: Coins and tokens

Phase	Context	Denomination	Date	Comments
–	Eval. Ditch 1006	*as* or *dupondius*	mid 1st to mid 3rd century	illegible
4b	Northern trackway ditch	*dupondius*	mid 1st to mid 3rd century	illegible
4b	Southern trackway ditch	*sestertius*	mid 1st to 2nd century	illegible
4b	Drying oven 5634	AE3	AD 330–5	GLORIA EXERCITUS 2 standards ?copy
–	subsoil	lead token	17th–18th century	design is on one face only. Probably initials 'JH'

Vessel glass

A single vessel glass fragment (n.i.), part of a handle attachment of natural green-coloured glass, was recovered from Ring Ditch 2, Phase 4b. The vessel form, a large cylindrical bottle, is represented on Roman sites of all types and is common between the 2nd and 3rd centuries AD (Price and Cottam 1998, 191–4).

Worked stone, by Fiona Roe

The worked stone objects amount to one quern and two quern/millstone fragments. None of the materials in use had travelled far, coming either from in or around the Forest of Dean or from the local area. Most notable among the stone finds is the quern fragment, which unfortunately is insufficiently complete to determine its original form. May Hill sandstone, originating either from quarries on May Hill itself, 24km to the south-west, or from the Malverns is utilised as a quern material from the Neolithic through to the Middle Iron Age. Occurrences of Iron Age date are commonplace both in the immediate area and further afield, and these are often associated with pottery tempered with Malvernian rock. The recovery of this quern fragment from a plough furrow 5102, a feature cutting the Middle Bronze Age ditches in Area A, raises the possibility of an early date. However, the presence, albeit limited, of Middle Iron Age and Roman material makes a later date perhaps most likely. The other two quern or millstone fragments, both of which derive from Roman contexts (Phase 4b) are Upper Old Red Sandstone from the Forest of Dean/ Wye Valley area, some 40–48km to the south-west.

n.i. May Hill sandstone fragment from quern with part of grinding surface. Weight 290g. Fill of plough furrow, Period 6.

n.i. Burnt fragment of Upper Old Red Sandstone, pebbly sandstone from a quern or millstone, probably upper stone with pitted top surface, possible raised rim. Weight 1070g. Enclosure 4 internal ditch. Phase 4b.

n.i. Upper Old Red Sandstone, pebbly sandstone fragment from quern or millstone, no working traces. Weight 160g. Enclosure 4 internal ditch. Phase 4b.

Building material, by E.R. McSloy and Fiona Roe

Ceramic building material

Small quantities (25 fragments, weighing 3525g) of ceramic building material were recovered. A total of 16 fragments derived from Period 4 deposits, with the remainder unstratified. The stratified material was found in ditch or pit fills in the north-eastern portion of the site or from the trackway (6 fragments). Material of certain Roman date included examples of tegula (3 fragments), imbrex (3 fragments) and brick (5 fragments). Further fragments of probable Roman material consisted of flat pieces, 15–20mm in thickness and probably from tegulae. All material occurred in a similar hard, sandy orange-brown coloured fabric.

The ceramic building material assemblage is small and clearly insufficient to imply the presence of a high-status building in the immediate area. Excavations at sites along the Eastern Relief Road produced similarly modest quantities and are unlikely to represent the source of this material (Walker et al. 2004). A possible origin for this material is the Oldbury district of Tewkesbury, where finds of painted plaster and roofing tiles suggest the presence of substantial buildings (Hannan 1993).

Stone

A total of 11 fragments (4778g) of building stone was recovered from Period 4 features. None of the probable roofing fragments retain nail/peg holes, or are sufficiently complete to determine original form. Four flat fragments, identifiable as Lower Old Red Sandstone originating from the Forest of Dean, probably represent roofing material. Six fragments occurring in the local lias included possible examples of roofing tile and paving in addition to miscellaneous block fragments. A single fragment was identifiable as Jurassic shelly limestone, the nearest source for which would be Bredon Hill.

THE BIOLOGICAL EVIDENCE

Human remains, by Malin Holst

Introduction

Eleven skeletons and six disarticulated assemblages of human bone dating to Periods 3, 4 and 5 were subjected to osteological analysis (Table 8). The aim of the skeletal analysis was to determine the age, sex and stature of the skeletons, as well as to record and diagnose any skeletal manifestations of disease and trauma. The preservation and completeness of the skeletons was assessed and their age, sex and stature determined. All pathological lesions were recorded and described. Full details of the skeletons, including photographs of significant palaeopathology, are contained in the archive.

Osteological analysis

Preservation and completeness

The majority of skeletons (46%) were moderately well preserved and showed limited evidence for erosion, but exhibited many post-mortem breaks. Three of the skeletons were in a good condition, exhibiting little erosion and few post-mortem breaks. Two skeletons were poorly preserved, with fragmentation of the bone into tiny pieces and this was much worse in two skeletons that were very badly preserved.

The shallow depth of burial, combined with truncation of some graves by post-medieval ploughing, had caused the loss of the majority of spongy bones, including the spines and joints. Additionally, many of the smaller bones such as fingers and toes had been lost. As a result the skeletons were only between 5% and 90% complete. Three disarticulated human bone fragments were femora. They belonged to an infant, a juvenile and an adolescent or adult.

The osteological analysis of the skeletal remains established that the assemblage included one late term foetus, four neonates, one infant, a juvenile, seven adult males and one middle-aged female. The majority of males were middle-aged adults, but a young adult and a mature adult were also identified. The evidence suggests that those individuals that survived birth and the first few months of life were likely to survive to middle age.

Palaeopathological analysis

Infectious disease

Evidence for infection was observed in SKs 2, 4, 8, 9 and 14. In all individuals, with the exception of SK 8, the infection was characterised by superficial inflammatory lesions on the surfaces of the tibiae. Tibiae are the most likely bones to show evidence for inflammation because they are more vulnerable to knocks than other parts of the body. In all five individuals the type of skeletal lesion (lamellar bone) observed suggested that the inflammation was receding at the time of death.

Inflammatory lesions on human bones can be indicative of infectious diseases, such as leprosy and syphilis, and of non-specific localised infection, such as varicose veins, leg ulcers or trauma to the shins. However, the lesions only form in the bone if the inflammation is chronic and long-standing (Roberts and Manchester 1995, 125). Evidence for infection was observed in a young adult male (SK 14, Phase 4b) and characterised by lamellar bone, a striated type of lesion, which is typical of infection that was receding at the time of death. The lamellar bone was observed on the pulmonary (lung) side of the sternal ends (the

Table 8: Catalogue of articulated and disarticulated human bone

SK No.	Position	Orientation	Grave goods	Feature type	Period/Phase	Preservation	Completeness	Age	Sex	Stature	No. of teeth present	Calculus	Caries	Abscesses	DEH	Infractions	Wear	Periodontitis
1	Flexed on left	N/S	–	Ditch	3	Good	85%	Neonate	–	–	10 decid	–	–	–	–	–	None	–
11	–	–	–	Grave pit	3	Moderate	70%	Neonate	–	–	1 decid	–	–	–	–	–	None	–
13	Flexed on right	S/N	–	Ditch	3	Moderate	45%	Neonate	–	–	9 decid	–	–	–	–	–	None	–
2	Flexed on left	N/S	–	Grave pit	4b	Poor	70%	36–45	M	173.9 ± 4.32cm	22 perm	20	2	2	1	1	Moderate	Moderate
3	–	N/S	–	Grave pit	4b	Very poor	7%	26–35	M	–	2 perm	1	–	–	–	–	Moderate	–
4	Flexed tightly on left	NE/SW	–	Grave pit	4b	Poor	50%	46+	M	–	16 perm	–	3	1	–	–	Severe	Moderate
10	Flexed on left	S/N	–	Grave pit	4b	Very poor	30%	36+	M	–	6 perm	–	2	–	–	–	Severe	–
12	Flexed on right	W/E	–	Grave pit	4b	Good	90%	Foetus	–	–	3 decid	–	–	–	–	–	None	–
14	–	–	–	Well	4b	Good	70%	16–20	M	166.85 ± 4.05cm	7 perm	7	–	–	1	–	Slight	–
8	Supine extended	S/N	–	Grave pit	5	Moderate	50%	36–45	M	–	–							
9	Supine extended	SW/NE	Y	Grave pit	5	Moderate	70%	36–45	F	–	–							

Table 8 (cont.): Catalogue of articulated and disarticulated human bone

SK No.	Position	Orientation	Grave goods	Feature type	Period/Phase	Preservation	Completeness	Age	Sex	Stature	No. of teeth present	Calculus	Caries	Abscesses	DEH	Infractions	Wear	Periodontitis
16	–	–	–	Holloway	4	–	5%	Adult	M	–	–	–	–	–	–	–	–	–
17	–	–	–	Gully 6195	4	–	5%	Neonate	–	–	–	–	–	–	–	–	–	–
6112	–	–	–	Disarticulated with SK 8	5	–	30%	Juvenile. Femoral shaft	–	–	–	–	–	–	–	–	–	–
5694	–	–	–	Ditch 3	3	–	23%	Infant. Proximal femur. (left side)	–	–	–	–	–	–	–	–	–	–
6045	–	–	–	Enclosure 1	2	–	10%	Adult? Femoral shaft	–	–	–	–	–	–	–	–	–	–
7021	–	–	–	Southern trackway ditch	4	–	15%	Adult. Femoral shaft	–	–	–	–	–	–	–	–	–	–

breastbone end) of all the ribs. Rib periostitis is thought to result from lung infections, such as pneumonia or tuberculosis. SK 14 also showed evidence for mild inflammatory lesions in the form of porosity on the outer part of the skull. This is indicative of a mild scalp inflammation, the cause of which could not be determined. However, the skeleton displayed destructive lesions of the hips, which may have been caused by tuberculosis.

Metabolic conditions
Two cases of metabolic condition were noted in this population. SK 4, a mature adult male, and SK 10, an old middle to mature adult male, exhibited *cribra orbitalia*, pitted lesions in the eye orbits. The lesions are thought to be indicative of periods of iron deficiency during childhood, but can be observed in both children and adults.

Degenerative joint disease
The most common type of joint disease observed tends to be degenerative joint disease (DJD). This condition is characterised by both bone formation (osteophytes) and bone resorption (porosity) at and around the articular surfaces of the joints, which can cause great discomfort and disability (Rogers 2001).

All the adults suffered from joint disease, with the exception of SK 14 and the very poorly preserved SK 3, a young middle adult male. The condition was least evident in SK 8; however, this was probably the result of extensive post-depositional joint loss, rather than actual lower prevalence. The left thumbs of this individual and SK 2 showed evidence for osteophyte formation (outgrowths of bone) indicative of joint degeneration. SK 10 exhibited evidence for slight osteophyte formation in the left shoulder and in the mandible joints. SK 2 and 4 suffered from mild DJD in the joints of the hips.

Three of the adults (SKs 4, 9 and 10) exhibited evidence for moderate joint disease in the spine. This was noted in the neck vertebrae of SKs 4 and 10 and the lower parts of the spine of SKs 4 and 9. The DJD in SK 10 was severe and in the case of SK 4, osteoarthritis was noted in the sacrum and the fifth lumbar vertebra. Spinal joint disease is common in most periods, affecting, for example, 14% of the Roman population (Roberts and Cox 2003, 145).

A different condition which affects the spine is Schmorl's nodes, indentations in the upper and lower surfaces of the vertebral bodies, most commonly in the lower thoracic vertebrae (Hilton *et al.* 1976). Schmorl's nodes can result from damage to the intervertebral discs, which then impinge onto the vertebral body surface (Rogers 2001), and may cause necrosis (death) of the surrounding tissue. Rupture of the discs only occurs if sufficient axial compressive forces are causing pressure on the central part of the discs; frequent lifting or carrying of heavy loads can cause this. Schmorl's nodes were observed between the tenth thoracic to the fourth lumbar vertebrae of SKs 3, 4 and 9 and were most severe in SK 9, the only female skeleton. Schmorl's nodes were also common in the Roman period, with a crude prevalence rate of 8.9% (Roberts and Cox 2003, 147).

Trauma
SK 10 exhibited a circular raised area on the outer surface of the skull, on the left part of the frontal, *c.* 6cm above the left orbit. The lesion was 20.5mm by 17.6mm in size and was raised by 5mm. It is probable that this lesion represents an ossified haematoma (a blood-clot that has become bone), which may be due to well-healed blunt force trauma that must have occurred some time before death. Whether the injury occurred accidentally or was deliberately inflicted could not be determined. However, the injury's position on the left part of

the man's forehead could be indicative of a right-handed attacker. The man obviously survived the injury for some time for the blood-clot to become bone. However, ossified haematomas tend to resolve after two years, suggesting that the injury was less than two years old.

SK 2, a middle-aged male, had also sustained severe trauma to the right arm. Careful reconstruction of the right elbow, which was fractured ante-mortem into numerous fragments and had subsequently suffered from severe post-mortem damage, succeeded in identifying the cause. It is likely that direct trauma to the right elbow had caused a Monteggia fracture of the radius and ulna (Dandy and Edwards 1998, 202), leading to dislocation of the radial head and fracture of the proximal third of the ulna, which was well-healed but mal-aligned anteriorly. Furthermore, a comminuted fracture of the distal humerus led to shattering of the elbow joint into numerous pieces. This meant that the radial head was misshapen, much enlarged, the proximal ulna was malformed and that some of the loose fragments had re-grown onto the distal humerus, making the joint into a claw-shape, rather than the usual rounded shape. This led to complete mal-alignment of the radius and ulna, meaning that it must have been impossible to use the forearm. This was confirmed by the lack of osteoarthritis in any of the joints, suggesting disuse of the arm. The seven loose bone fragments in the elbow would have made recovery even less likely and might have caused mechanical locking of the elbow joint (ibid., 199, 375). The injury may also have led to stretching of the ulnar nerve, causing tardy ulnar palsy (ibid., 362). This can cause tingling, pain, numbness of the hand and also 'claw hand', as well as wasting of the muscles.

The same individual also exhibited a finger fracture, which was well-healed and may have been related. He also showed evidence for severe muscular trauma to the ligament connecting the tibia and fibula in the right lower leg, at the ankle joint. This suggests that he either experienced several episodes of trauma that affected his right side, or that one major accident had caused all of the injuries observed. It is likely that this man would have been partly disabled, which may have affected his role in society.

Occasionally, it is possible to infer trauma to the soft tissue on the bones, in the form of ligamentous or muscular trauma. This is expressed through the formation of bony processes (enthesopathies) at the site of ligament attachments. Additionally, it is possible to observe bone defects at the site of muscle insertions, which are the result of constant micro-trauma and are usually activity-related (Hawkey and Merbs 1995, 334). The majority of muscular trauma was noted in the legs. Some muscular arm trauma was, however, observed.

As discussed above, SK 2 suffered form a large enthesopathy to the interosseous ligament that holds the right tibia and fibula together. It is probable that the individual was involved in an accident, such as a trip or fall, that caused damage to the ligament.

Osteochondritis dissecans

Circular cortical defects were seen in the distal joint surfaces of the scapulae of SK 14 and on the right knee (distal femur) of SK 8. While the shoulder joint lesions were small (3.7mm by 2mm), the knee lesion was very large (16.5mm in diameter) and consisted of an irregular central depression. It is probable that these defects are *osteochondritis dissecans* lesions. This condition is characterised by necrosis of part of the joint area, with separation of a small bone fragment from the joint surface, which can then become disconnected and remain as a loose body within the joint capsule or may be resorbed or become reattached. *Osteochondritis dissecans* is most commonly observed at the knee, ankle and elbow (Aufderheide and Rodríguez-Martín 1998, 82). The condition tends to have little effect in adolescents, who are most likely to suffer from it. Adults with the condition, on the other hand, can suffer pain, interlocking and instability of the joint (Clanton and DeLee 1982, 59). The initiating mechanism for *osteochondritis* is now thought to be multifactoral and related to trauma at a susceptible location (Frederico *et al.* 1990).

Dental disease

Most of the jaws were incomplete as a result of post-depositional factors and neither of the two Anglo-Saxon skeletons (SKs 8 and 9) had skulls or teeth. No teeth were recovered from the disarticulated bone assemblage (Table 8). As the majority of teeth derived from the undated or Roman skeletons, the prevalence rates for dental disease was compared with that for the Roman period.

All four foetal and neonatal skeletons (SKs 1, 12, 13 and 15) had some deciduous teeth, which were the tips of the developing tooth crowns in all cases. A total of 23 tooth crowns survived. The majority of these were maxillary teeth. As expected, none of these developing teeth displayed any pathology.

Of the five adults with teeth, with a total of 72 tooth positions present, 53 teeth were recovered. Eleven teeth had been lost ante-mortem, while a further eight teeth had been lost post-mortem. Almost all of the ante-mortem tooth loss was observed in SK 10, an old middle to mature adult male with severe caries (cavities). It is likely that the severe tooth loss was caused by the cavities.

Dental wear tends to be more common and severe in archaeological populations than in modern teeth. Severity of the dental wear was assessed using a chart developed by Smith (1984). The surviving teeth showed a clear correlation between age and the severity of the dental wear: the teeth of the mature adults (SKs 4 and 10) exhibited severe wear, those of the middle adults (SKs 2 and 3) moderate wear and the young adult (SK 14) had little dental wear.

Discussion

The skeletal remains were in a very poor to good condition and largely incomplete. The demographic data together with the palaeopathological evidence suggests that the risk of dying was greatest around the time of birth. This may have been due to complications in late pregnancy or during birth, as well as inadequate aftercare, infection or inadequate infant nutrition. Those individuals that survived the first year of childhood were likely to live to middle age. The adult skeletons displayed little evidence that suggested hardship during childhood with the exception of two individuals who displayed lesions on the teeth indicative of arrested growth as a result of disease or malnutrition during the first seven years of childhood. Two further individuals had lesions in the eye orbits indicative of childhood anaemia.

Evidence for trauma to those muscles responsible for the legs and hip was noted in all adults. This, together with the joint disease noted in the mature adults, as well as injuries to the spines of SKs 2, 3 and 9 suggests that these people carried out physically demanding activities. It is likely that involvement in these activities began in the late teens and was continued throughout life. The inflammatory lesions observed on the shins of five of the adults were probably also caused through work-related incidents, such as bumps or ulcers.

It is possible that a work-related accident caused the injuries observed in a middle-aged male (SK 2). This individual suffered from severe trauma to the right elbow, causing fracture of the elbow into tiny fragments, dislocation of the radius and fracture of the forearm, locking of the elbow and subsequent disuse of the right arm. The same individual also had a broken right finger, a ligament injury to the right ankle and chipped teeth. All the injuries were healed, suggesting that they had occurred some time before death.

SK 10, a middle-aged or mature adult male, had suffered an injury to his left forehead that might have been caused by interpersonal violence. The individual had a blood clot on the forehead above the left orbit that had become bone. Although the injury had not occurred immediately before death, it was less than two years old.

Age-related disease was observed in three of the older individuals (SKs 2, 4 and 10) who suffered from joint disease of the spine and hips. More severe joint disease in the form of osteoarthritis was noted in the neck of SK 4.

Generally, infectious disease was relatively rare in Roman populations in Britain, probably because the lack of dense settlements prior to the Roman period meant that infectious diseases had not been able to spread easily. It is only in the Roman period that the first cases of tuberculosis (Roberts and Cox 2003) and leprosy (Roberts 2002, 213) have been recorded.

A young adult male, SK 14, exhibited numerous inflammatory rib lesions, which were healing at death and were probably caused by pneumonia or tuberculosis. The same individual also showed evidence for hip infection, which could potentially have been caused by tuberculosis and this appears to correlate with a higher prevalence of tuberculosis in Roman Gloucestershire compared with that in other parts of the country (Roberts and Cox 2003, 11, 119). Roberts and Cox found a prevalence rate of 0.2% of tuberculosis overall for the Roman period, with individuals affected coming from Dorset, Hampshire, Lincolnshire and Gloucestershire.

Animal bone, by Sylvia Warman

Methodology
The Period 1 assemblage is too weathered and fragmented to warrant further analysis but is discussed in relation to the relative contributions of wild and domestic taxa. The methodology for the Period 3/4 assemblage identified animal bones from secure contexts to element and species. The information was collated using an access database and included; element, species, size, sex, weight, parts present (using the Dobney and Rielly 1988 zonation system), fusion (for ageing estimates following Silver 1969), tooth wear (for age estimates following Grant 1982), pathology, burning, butchery and weathering (following Behrensmeyer 1978). Sheep were distinguished from goat using the criteria recommended by Payne (1985). Whole long bones were measured to enable the calculation of withers heights following von den Driesch and Boessneck (1974). The numbers of animals represented by the assemblage were estimated using both NISP (number of identified specimens) and MNI (minimum number of individuals). The range and proportions of the species present as well as the age profiles for the most numerous domesticates were compared with other assemblages of similar date in the area.

Results

Period 1: Middle Bronze Age (mid 2nd millennium BC)
The assemblage from Ditches 1 and 2 comprised 882 fragments from 722 bones weighing 6.7kg. A quarter could be identified to species (Table 9). Ditch 5314 yielded smaller

Table 9: Animal bone from Period 1

Feature	No. of fragments	No. of bones	Weight (gms)	No. of bones ID to species	Large mammal	Small mammal	Mandibles	Epiphyses	Species/part	State	Age
Ditch 1 disuse	480	408	3589	185	3	–	2	16	RD(MTP) B(H,V,UL,LL,MP) O/C(H,LL,MP) S(H,UL) D(H) CSZ(H,V,R,UL,LB) SSZ(UL,LB,LL) UNID(F)	BT MB WE BT GN RT BN	A, SA, I
Ditch 2 use	26	21	171	2	2	–	–	–	B(H,LL) CSZ(V,LB) SSZ(LB)	WE GN RT BN	A
Ditch 2 disuse	293	229	1796.5	26	3	–	3	8	B(H,UL,LL,MTP,P) O/C(H,LL) S(H,UL) CSZ(MP,R,V,LB) SSZ(H,R,P,LB,F) UNID(F)	WE MB BN GN BT RT	A, J
Ditch 5413 disuse	83	64	1165.3	9	2	1	2	–	RD(ANT) B(H) O/C(H) S(H) CSZ(LB) SSZ(LB) SM(LB) UNID(F)	WE BN MB BT	A
Totals	**882**	**722**	**6721.8**	**222**	**3**	**1**	**7**	**24**			

Key to codes
Mandibles = simple count
Epiphyses = simple count
Large mammal and small mammal scores: 1–10 fragments = 1, 10–100 fragments = 2, 100+ fragments = 3
Species: B = *Bos taurus* (cow), O/C *Ovis/Capra* (sheep/goat), S = *Sus scrofa* (pig), D = *Canis familiaris* (dog), CSZ = cow-sized, SSZ = sheep-sized, SM small mammal (mouse-sized), UNID = unidentified.
Parts: ANT = antler, H = head, HC = horncore, V = vertebra, R = rib, UL = upper limb, LL = lower limb, MP = metapodial, P = phalange, FB = flat bone, LB = long bone, F = fragment.
State: WE = weathered, BT = butchery marks, BN = burnt, GN = gnawed, RT = root etching, MB = modern break, PA = pathology.
Age: F/N = foetal/neonatal, I = infant, J = juvenile, SA = sub–adult, A = adult, O = old adult.

55

quantities of material. All the bone showed significant weathering indicating some level of exposure prior to deposition evidenced by dog gnawing. Species identified included both domestic and wild taxa: cattle, sheep/goat, pig, dog and red deer. No meat-bearing bones from wild species were present. The domestic species included both non-meat and meat bearing elements. Butchery evidence was present on animal bone from the fills of all three features.

Periods 3 and 4: Late Iron Age/Early Roman to Roman (1st to 4th century AD)
Hand collected animal bones from the two periods totalled 1753 fragments from 810 bones weighing 32kg (Table 10). A further 333 fragments from 315 bones weighing 83g were recovered from the processed samples (Table 11). The Period 3 assemblage derived from linear ditch fills (Ditches 3, 4, 6, and 7068) and Enclosures 2 and 3, including curvilinear Ditch 15. Much of the Period 4 assemblage was recovered from the deposits within the well, with a small quantity from posthole 6782 near the well and ditches associated with Enclosures 9, 11 and 12.

The animal bone included large and small mammals, birds and amphibians. The range and variety of domestic species increased during Periods 3 and 4 to include chicken and horse, with preservation markedly better (see Table 10). The most common species was cattle, followed by sheep/goat and sheep. All have high MNIs. Horse, pig and dog are present in small numbers, while raven (*Corvus corvax*) was represented by the right and left mandibles from two sides of the lower jaw (ditch 7033). Two toad bones (*Bufo sp*) were identified from Ditch 4. The well yielded a wide range of species in a very good state of preservation including several near complete individuals of sheep and fox and a humerus from a member of the thrush family (*Turdus* sp.). Animal bone recovered from processed environmental samples included cattle, sheep/goat, pig, fox, weasel, mouse, shrew, field vole, vole sp., rodent, frog and frog/toad.

Tooth wear and fusion
Mandible wear scores (MWS) were calculated using Grant (1982) and, along with fusion tables, are contained in the site archive. Those sheep/goat with MWS above 28/30 are fully adult with the third molar erupted and would be aged 2–3 years or older. For this assemblage 56% of sheep/goat fulfilled these criteria. The fusion data for sheep/goat suggested that a substantial proportion were slaughtered shortly after reaching one year old, suggesting an emphasis on meat production. Those specimens securely identified as sheep (following criteria of Boessneck 1969) show a slightly different pattern with a larger proportion of individuals kept into adulthood, possibly for wool and milk production. However this pattern may reflect the fact that a large number of elements probably come from a single individual from the well.

For cattle, following Grigson (1982), a MWS of 30 would equate to an adult over 3 years. Of the cattle 57% are adult and therefore over 3 years old. The fusion data for cattle is consistent with cattle being killed for meat with some retained into adulthood for other purposes such as dairy, traction or breeding. For pig a MWS of 27 would indicate that all teeth are erupted, equating to an age in excess of 18 months. Both pig mandibles recovered were younger than 18 months. None of the pig bones encountered were fused, suggesting culling at an early age which is entirely consistent with a species kept purely for meat.

Table 10: Identified hand-collected animal bone from Periods 3 and 4

MNI=Minimum Number of Individuals; NISP = Number of Identified Specimens

Element	Horse	Cattle	Sheep /Goat	Sheep	Goat	Pig	Fox/ Dog	Dog	Fox	Vole	Rodent	Chicken	Thrush	Raven	Toad	Frog
Skull + horncore	–	1	–	4	–	–	–	–	–	–	–	–	–	–	–	–
Skull	3	17	9	13	1	2	–	2	3	1	–	–	–	–	–	–
Horncore	–	1	–	3	1	–	–	1	–	–	–	–	–	–	–	–
Maxilla	–	7	2	3	–	2	–	4	3	–	–	–	–	–	–	–
Upper teeth	6	43	45	–	–	–	–	2	–	–	–	–	–	–	–	–
Mandible	3	48	34	9	–	10	–	1	3	–	–	–	–	2	–	–
Lower teeth	17	41	40	–	–	11	–	3	1	–	1	–	–	–	–	–
Hyoid	–	–	1	–	–	–	–	–	–	–	–	–	–	–	–	–
Atlas	–	2	2	1	–	–	–	–	–	–	–	–	–	–	–	–
Axis	–	1	1	–	–	–	–	–	1	–	–	–	–	–	–	–
Vertebrae	–	–	–	–	–	–	–	–	5	–	–	–	–	–	–	1
Rib	–	–	–	–	–	–	–	–	13	–	–	–	–	–	–	–
Scapula	1	11	–	1	–	3	–	–	3	–	–	–	–	–	–	1
Humerus	2	4	12	3	–	3	–	–	4	–	–	–	1	–	–	–
Radius	6	18	8	2	–	2	–	–	2	–	–	–	–	–	–	–
Ulna	4	9	–	–	–	1	–	1	4	–	–	1	–	–	–	1
Carpal	–	6	1	–	–	–	–	–	–	–	–	–	–	–	–	–
Metacarpal	6	18	3	4	–	1	2	–	–	–	–	–	–	–	–	–
Innominate	7	18	2	1	–	2	–	2	3	–	–	–	–	–	–	2
Sacrum	–	–	–	–	–	–	–	–	–	–	–	–	–	–	–	–
Femur	4	10	5	2	–	–	–	–	5	–	–	–	–	–	1	1
Patella	–	–	1	1	–	–	–	–	–	–	–	–	–	–	–	–
Tibia	5	15	4	2	–	2	–	–	3	–	–	–	–	–	2	4
Fibula	–	1	–	–	–	–	–	–	–	–	–	–	–	–	–	–
Talus	4	5	2	–	–	1	–	–	–	–	–	–	–	–	–	–
Calcaneus	3	9	–	–	–	1	–	–	–	–	–	–	–	–	–	–
Tarsal	–	4	3	–	–	–	–	–	–	–	–	–	–	–	–	–
Metatarsal	2	14	9	2	–	–	–	–	4	–	–	–	–	–	–	–

Table 10 (cont.): Identified hand-collected animal bone from Periods 3 and 4

MNI=Minimum Number of Individuals; NISP = Number of Identified Specimens

Element	Horse	Cattle	Sheep/Goat	Sheep	Goat	Pig	Fox/Dog	Dog	Fox	Vole	Rodent	Chicken	Thrush	Raven	Toad	Frog
Metapodial	3	5	3	–	–	1	–	1	–	–	–	–	–	–	–	–
Sessamoid	–	3	3	–	–	–	–	–	–	–	–	–	–	–	–	–
1st phalanx	3	14	7	2	–	1	–	–	–	–	–	–	–	–	–	–
2nd phalanx	–	10	–	–	–	3	–	–	1	–	–	–	–	–	–	–
3rd phalanx	–	5	–	–	–	–	–	–	–	–	–	–	–	–	–	–
NISP totals	79	342	195	52	2	46	2	17	58	1	1	1	1	2	3	8
Total weight	8644	19553	1251	870.7	127	783.5	1.5	211	255.8	0.1	0.05	2	0.1	3	0.8	0.36
MNI	7	23	16	8	1	9	1	5	3	1	1	1	1	1	2	2
% by NISP	9.75	42.2	24.07	6.42	0.25	5.68	0.25	2.1	7.16	0.12	0.12	0.12	0.12	0.25	0.12	1
% by weight	27.26	61.67	3.94	2.75	0.4	2.47	0.005	0.67	0.81	0.0003	0.0002	0.006	0.0003	0.003	0.003	0.001

Table 11: Identified sieved animal bone from Periods 3 and 4

MNI=Minimum Number of Individuals; NISP = Number of Identified Specimens

Taxon	MNI	NISP	No. of bones	No. of fragments	Weight (g)
Cattle	2	4	4	5	**60.90**
Sheep/Goat	7	25	25	29	**13.20**
Pig	1	2	2	2	**1.30**
Fox	1	12	12	12	**2.00**
Weasel	1	1	1	1	**0.05**
Field Vole	4	11	11	23	**0.43**
Vole sp	5	14	14	14	**0.38**
Mouse sp	1	3	3	3	**0.11**
Shrew	2	3	3	3	**0.09**
Rodent	2	3	3	3	**0.09**
Frog	27	217	217	218	**3.94**
Frog/Toad	10	20	20	20	**0.41**
Totals	*63*	*315*	*315*	*333*	**82.90**

Sexing

Most specimens could not be sexed. Certain diagnostic elements such as teeth, pelvis, horn core and atlas can be an aid to sexing. Pigs were sexed using the canine teeth. Four males and one female were identified. A cattle acetabulum was recorded as male (following Grigson 1982). Two horse canines were sexed, and found to be male. The fully identified sheep material was sufficiently well preserved for elements to be sexed as six female and one male. These seven bones were all from deposits within the well and the female ones may have been from a single individual.

Withers heights

Whole long bones of domestic stock were measured and multiplication factors (von den Driesch and Bosseneck 1974) used to estimate withers height (the height of quadrupeds at the shoulder). Horses ranged from 12 to 14 hands. The range of withers height for sheep was 543–63mm. A single cattle tibia produced a withers height of 1190mm.

Pathology

Pathological changes were observed in less than 1% of the assemblage. The most prevalent pathologies were an advanced form of gum (periodontal) disease and calculus formation (mineralised plaque) in the mandibles or teeth of sheep/goat. A juvenile sheep skull fragment may have derived from a four-horned type (such as the Hebridean breed). The horn cores were quite rudimentary, and this trait may represent a congenital abnormality. Other observed pathologies included a missing distal loop from a third molar of a cattle mandible. This may be an inherited abnormality. Additional bone growth on a horse tibia towards the ankle and a healed fracture on a frog tibio-fibula were other recognisable pathologies.

Bone modification and taphonomic changes

The incidence of butchery marks in the assemblage is low to moderate at 7%. These mostly consisted of shafts of long bones which had been chopped through, possibly for the extraction of marrow. Chop marks and cut marks were also seen. Butchered species included cattle, sheep/goat, pig and horse. Around 6% of specimens showed signs of gnawing, all but one by dogs. Weathering was observed in 13% of the assemblage. Most specimens were scored as 1 or 2 on Behrensmeyer's (1978) scale, indicating that the weathering was not severe.

Discussion

The animal bone assemblage from Period 1 reflects the use of some wild taxa alongside the domestic species which were presumably the main source of meat. The species present and relative proportions show some similarities with the small assemblages recovered from the Eastern Relief Road sites (Hambleton 2004), where cattle were identified as the main provider of meat in this period.

Within the Period 3 assemblage the presence of chicken confirmed the domestic use of this species. It is currently believed to have been introduced to Britain during the Late Iron Age (Davis 1987). The occurrence of the two raven mandibles is interesting, given that this is a carrion feeder and not a game species. The raven occupied a significant place in Celtic mythology associated with both death and war (Green 1998, 87, 177). Given the presence of both raven and chicken in the Period 3 assemblage it is interesting to note that the Period 4 deposits do not contain any domestic birds; the only bird species present was a humerus from the genus *Turdus* (thrush/blackbird family).

Cattle and sheep/goat were the main providers of meat. The wide range of species amongst the Period 4 material reflects the presence of wild and commensurable species and the dominance of the well assemblage. It is likely that the well may have acted as a 'pit-fall' trap - hence the presence of the frogs/toads, small mammals and foxes. The domestic carcasses, especially limb bones from a single sheep, may represent a defective or diseased animal discarded after the well went out of use, or became contaminated, or be deliberate placement. The two lower fills of the well (7144 and 7135) produced very rich assemblages of hand collected and sieved animal bones. The animal bone recovered from 7144 comprised one cow, at least one sheep, at least two sheep/goat, one pig, one dog/fox, one field vole, one vole sp., one blackbird/thrush, at least 12 frogs, one toad and four frog/toad. The sheep bones included a front limb from a single individual. Only the cattle tibia showed signs of butchery and the pig hip had been gnawed by dogs.

Fill 7135 produced a large assemblage of animal bones representing at least three cattle, two horses, two goats, four sheep, three sheep/goat and a pig as well as rodents and frogs/toads. The horse bones included two cannon bones from a single individual, sheep bones were common and although a minimum of four individuals were present the majority of the bones are from two partial skeletons: a juvenile and a sub-adult. Significant parts of three fox skeletons were also present. Like the sheep these are very well preserved and show no signs of butchery. The sheep and fox carcasses must have been deposited rapidly with flesh still attached, evidenced by the lack of weathering and gnawing marks and the high degree of articulation. The damp silt and anaerobic conditions provided an environment that resulted in very good preservation of animal bone and the characteristic dark brown colour and smooth surface. The smaller species, weasel and rodents, may have fallen into the well whereas the sheep and foxes must have been deliberately placed there. This may have been through a desire to dispose of vermin or infected meat, although consideration should also be given to this being a structured deposit 'closing' the well at the end of its period of use. The species of small mammal present suggest that the immediate environment around the site was grassland as the field vole favours rough meadows, with scrub and hedges providing cover for the weasel.

The animal bone recovered from the upper fills of the well, 6790, 6791 and 6792 contrasted with that from 7135 and 7144. The bones from the upper fills comprised butchery and household waste and there are no articulating joints or significant parts of carcasses. Gnawing and weathering was also more common, indicating exposure prior to burial.

The cattle mandible tooth wear evidence from Periods 3 and 4 suggests that meat production was the main focus, while the sheep/goat tooth wear data can be explained in a number of ways. One possibility is that individuals had reached the desired age for slaughter and had been sent to market. This would support the obvious interpretation that the enclosure was involved with agricultural production, and we may note that the small mammal and insect data from the well indicates the proximity of meadow pasture. The second explanation is that animals over one year old were kept for secondary products such as milk or wool, and that the aged mandibles represent surplus young (especially males) and older individuals at the end of their productive life. The data for pig was more limited but the mandible wear scores fit with slaughter at a young age prior to dental maturity as would expected in a species kept entirely for meat production. The fusion data generally showed similar trends to the tooth wear data. Cattle were raised for meat with some individuals reaching skeletal maturity kept for breeding or secondary products. Sheep/goat showed a peak in individuals around a year old, suggesting that they were kept primarily for meat. Sheep show a greater number of adults, indicating a focus on secondary products, but caution must be used here as only fully fused adult long bones can be confidently identified as sheep or goat rather than a mixture of the two species (Boessneck 1969). Where neonatal cattle and sheep remains are found this is usually taken as evidence for stock-rearing. The fusion data for pig is consistent with the animals being slaughtered once the desired weight was achieved and no fully adult individuals are present. This may be due to the small sample size but some older breeding specimens would be expected unless piglets were imported from producer sites and simply fattened at this location. Pork is widely referred to as a Roman dish of choice in textual sources, but few archaeological bone assemblages bear out the level of exploitation indicated in the texts (Dobney 2001).

Comparable sites
The animal bone assemblages from Periods 3 and 4 are sufficiently sizeable and well preserved to permit comparison with other reported assemblages from the region. The species present are similar to those found on the Eastern Relief Road sites (Hambleton 2004); Bank Farm, Dumbleton and Elm Farm, Beckford, Worcestershire to the north (Higbee 2006), and Hucclecote further south near Gloucester (Stickler 2003). The predominance of cattle is a feature of all these assemblages.

At Elm Farm there was a peak kill-off of cattle at 3.5–4 years, with a smaller number killed before 2.5 years, whereas at Hucclecote all cattle age groups were represented equally. At the Eastern Relief Road sites cattle were primarily raised for meat, with a small proportion of adult stock kept for breeding and secondary products. Turning to sheep, at Hucclecote the tooth wear data indicated that 70% of sheep teeth came from mature animals, and the fusion data indicated ages between 2.5 and 3.5 years. A single new born specimen was also present. At Elm Farm the peak kill-off for sheep based on fusion data was 1.5–3 years, with few animals killed as lambs. The tooth wear data was broadly similar. The sheep evidence from Elm Farm is comparable to that found at Rudgeway Lane and the Eastern Relief Road sites. At the Eastern Relief Road sites the pig assemblage was dominated by adolescents, with few adults, and one foetal bone. This is in contrast to the situation here where no neonatal specimens of pig were found, and Hucclecote where the pig teeth were entirely from young animals.

The evidence for butchery varies from 1 to 2% at the Relief Road sites and Hucclecote, 7% here, 16% at Bank Farm and 30% at Elm Farm. Pathologies relating to tooth and gum problems comprised less than 1% of the assemblage here, whilst some specimens from Hucclecote showed joint disease.

The size of livestock at Rudgeway Lane obtained from withers height calculations is comparable to the range recorded in other local assemblages. It may be that the smaller 'Celtic' horse continued to be bred, but that a larger breed was introduced during the Roman period. The number of specimens involved is very small, however, so this must remain conjecture until a greater number of well-dated horse long bones are recovered from Iron Age and Roman deposits on similar sites.

The animal bone assemblage from Walton Cardiff follows the same trends as the comparable assemblages. The assemblages at all of these sites are dominated by cattle, kept primarily for meat. Sheep are also an important livestock largely kept for meat, but with a few older specimens hinting at the use of secondary products. The pig remains from Walton Cardiff are from juvenile and sub-adult specimens, matching the pattern seen throughout the sites reviewed above. In terms of size of individuals, cattle and sheep are of comparable size to those from the other sites. The size range of horses is similar to that seem at Bank Farm with both a smaller type and a medium-sized type present. The incidence of butchered bones is more variable between sites with Walton Cardiff at the lower end of the range and Elm Farm showing a greater proportion. The incidence of pathology is low at all sites, never exceeding 2%.

Conclusion

The animal bone from the site shows a relatively narrow range of species, the majority of which are domestic. Use of wild animals for meat and raw materials is evident in the Bronze Age but not in the Late Iron Age and Roman assemblages where domestic mammal remains are dominant. Animal husbandry must have been a significant element of the economy in Periods 3 and 4 and the multiple enclosures are indicative of stock raising. The small mammals and insects recorded from the base of the well indicate a local environment of rough pasture. Unfortunately the poor recovery and preservation of plant remains means that the arable element of the economy cannot be confirmed and compared to the faunal data. The fills of three ditches (Ditches 1, 2 and Trackway 1/Enclosure Ditch 4) and gullies, pits and postholes were subject to bioarchaeological assessment, but the results were poor in plant remains and no further analysis was recommended (CA 2006, 78).

The insect remains, by Emma Tetlow

The Phase 4b well lay in the south-eastern corner of Enclosure 9 close to a roundhouse and hearths (see Figs 7, 9, 10). Samples from the well were processed using the standard method of paraffin flotation outlined in Kenward *et al.* 1980. The insect remains were then sorted from the paraffin flot and the sclerites identified under a low power binocular microscope at x10 magnification. Where possible, the insect remains were identified by comparison with specimens in the Gorham and Girling collections housed at the University of Birmingham. The taxonomy used for the Coleoptera (beetles) follows that of Lucht 1987.

The assemblage

The sample from the primary fill (7144) produced an exceptionally well-preserved and interpretable assemblage which provides information not only on the environments immediately surrounding the well and activities within the enclosure, but also the wider landscape surrounding the enclosure system (Table 12).

A significant component of the assemblage is taxa found on dry, open ground, including the Carabidae or ground beetles. Most this group is found on sandy, sparsely vegetated ground (xerophilous taxa). Further species of ground beetle are found in association with specific vegetation, particularly sparsely vegetated and weed dominated scrub with stress tolerant and ruderal forbs (i.e. herbaceous taxa other than grass). The ground beetles *Harpalus aeneus* and *Amara similata* are associated with disturbed and waste ground colonised by a variety of ruderal herbaceous species (Koch 1989a; Lindroth 1974; 1986). *Harpalus rufipes* feeds upon the seeds of fat hen (Chenopodium album) and various knapweeds (Polygonum spp.),

Table 12: Insect species identified from the well

Context 7144 Sample no. 213 Volume 2 litres Weight 3kg		Context 7144 (cont.) Sample no. 213 (cont.) Volume 2 litres Weight 3kg	
Latin/Common Name	No.	Latin/Common Name	No.
COLEOPTERA (beetles)		Cercyon analis (Payk.)	12
Carabidae (ground beetles, tiger beetles)		Cercyon spp.	16
Nebria spp.	1	Megasternum boletophagum (Marsh.)	4
Notiophilus palustris (Duft.)	1	Cryptopleurum minutum (F.)	12
Notiophilus spp.	1		
Loricera pilicornis (F.)	2	Histeridae (carrion beetles)	
Trechus quadristriatus (Schrk)/striatulus Putzeys.	2	Kissister minimus (Aube)	2
Trechus spp.	9	Hister bissexstriatus F.	1
Bembidion guttula (F.)	1		
Bembidion spp. spring tail	4	Orthoperidae (minute fungus beetle)	
Harpalus azureus (F.)	2	Coryopholous cassidoides (Marsh.)	5
Harpalus rufipes (Geer.) strawberry seed beetle	2		
Harpalus aeneus (F.)	3	Staphylinidae (rove beetles)	
Harpalus rubripes (Duft.)	1	Phylodrepa florialis (Payk.)	3
Harpalus spp. strawberry seed beetle	20	Olophrum spp.	1
Pterostichus anthracinus (Ill.)	1	Oxytelus sculptus Grav.	4
Pterostichus spp. black clock	3	Oxytelus rugosus (F.)	5
Calathus fuscipes (Goeze.)	10	Oxytelus complanatus Er.	10
Calathus spp.	17	Oxytelus tetracarinatus (Block.)	4
Amara similata (Gyll.)	1	Oxytelus spp.	4
Amara lunicollis Schdte.	1	Platystethus arenarius (Fourcr.)	3
Amara eurynota (Panz.)	2	Platystethus nitens (Salhb.)	2
Amara convexisucula (Marsh.)	1	Platystethus spp.	7
Amara spp. sun beetles	15	Lathrobium spp.	1
Badister bipustulatus (F.)	2	Stenus spp.	1
Microlestes maurus (Sturm.)	4	Paedarus spp.	5
		Stilicus spp.	6
Hydraenidae (small water beetles)		Philonthus spp.	14
Hydraena spp.	1	Staphylinus spp.	2
Limnebius spp.	2	Ocypus olens Devil's coach horse beetle	2
Helophorus spp. Wheat mud beetle	15	Quedius spp.	3
		Leptacinus linearis (Grav.)	9
Hydrophilidae (scavenger water beetles)		Xantholinus spp.	13
Sphaeridium scarabaeoides (L.)	2	Tachyporus spp.	7
Cercyon haemorrhoidalis (F.)	1	Tachinus rufipes (Geer.)	1
Cercyon cf. tristis (Ill.)	10	Tachinus spp.	3
Cercyon sternalis Shp.	20	Tachyusa spp.	2
		Aleocharinae gen. & spp. Indet.	10

Table 12 (cont.): Insect species identified from the well

Context 7144 (cont.) Sample no. 213 (cont.) Volume 2 litres Weight 3kg		Context 7144 (cont.) Sample no. 213 (cont.) Volume 2 litres Weight 3kg	
Latin/Common Name	**No.**	**Latin/Common Name**	**No.**
Elateridae (click beetles)		Chrysomelidae (leaf beetles)	
Agriotes obscurus (L.)	2	Hydrothassa spp.	1
Agriotes spp.	1	Phylotreta spp.	41
Adelocera murina (L.)	1	Gastroidea viridula (Geer.)	1
Athousspp.	4	Haltica lythri Aube.	13
		Derocrepis rufipes (L.)	1
Cryptophagidae (silken fungus beetles)		Chaetocnema concinna (Marsh.) beet flea beetle	8
Atomaria spp. pygmy beetle	2	Chaetocnema spp. Beet flea beetle	10
		Psylliodes spp.cabbage beetles	12
Lathridiidae (mould beetles)			
Encimus minutus	9	Curculionidae (weevils)	
Corticaria spp.	4	Apion Limonii Kirby	3
		Apion aeneum (F.)	7
Cantharidae (soldier beetles)		Apion urticarium (Hbst.)	6
Cantharis spp.	1	Apion spp. Seed weevils	16
		Sitona cylindricollis (Fahrs.)	1
Anthicidae (monoceros beetle)		Sitona humeralis Steph.	1
Anthicus spp.	2	Sitona spp. Pea and been weevil	8
		?Hypera zoilus (scop.) clover leaf weevil	3
Scarabaeidae (dung beetles)		Ceutorhynchus contractus (Marsh.) cabbage leaf weevil	1
Geotrupes spp. (dor beetles)	100	Ceutorhynchus erysimi (F.)	2
Onthophagus joannae Goljan.	1	Ceutorhynchus sulcicollis (Payk.)	2
Onthophagus spp,	2	Ceutorhynchus asperifoliarum (Gyll.)	4
Oxymous silvestris (Scop.)	1	Ceutoryhnchus spp. Cabbage weevil	2
Aphodius rufipes (L.)	3	Cidnorhinus quadrimaculatus (L.) small nettle weevil	1
Aphodius luridus (F.)	5		
Aphodius sphacelatus (Panz.) or Aphodius prodromus (Brahm.)	5	Gymnetron pascuorum (Gyll.)	1
Aphodius ater (Geer.)	3	Gymnetron spp. Brookline gull weevil	2
Aphodus granarius (L.)	1		
Aphodius spp.	21	Hemiptera (true bugs)	4

while *Amara convexiscula* is more closely associated with fat hen, particularly in coastal environments. Both herbaceous taxa are weeds of arable crops which occur on waste and disturbed ground. Recent research suggests that fat hen may have been a cultivar during the later prehistoric period (Stace 1991; Stokes and Rowley Conwy 2002).

Other phytophagous (plant-eating) beetles recorded are also associated with plants commonly found in both waste and disturbed ground, including the Curculionidae (weevils) *Apion urticarium* and *Cidnorhinus quadrimaculatus* which are both found on nettles (*Urtica* spp.). *Apion aeneum* is found on mallows (Malvaceae), in waysides and hedgerow and *Gymetron pascuorum* on plantains (*Plantago* spp.) (Bullock 1993). The leaf beetle (chrysomelid) *Haltica lythri* was particularly abundant and is found on willow herbs (*Chamerion angustifolium* and *Epilobium* spp.) (Koch 1989b). These taxa therefore all indicate the presence of open, disturbed, 'weedy' vegetation.

Large numbers of Scarabaeidae (dung beetles) were also present, with *Geotrupes* spp. (the Dor beetle) particularly abundant. None of the dung beetles recovered are specific to a particular beast although some, such as *Aphodius rufipes*, *Aphodius granarius* and *Aphodius luridus*, prefer the dung of cattle and horses (Jessop 1986; Koch 1989b). Beetles associated with rotting manure and other foul decaying organic material were also identified, including small numbers of rove beetles (Staphylinidae) which include several species of the Oxyteline association, *Phylodrepa florialis*, *Xantholinus linearis* and *Ocypus olens* (Kenward and Hall 1995) and the scavenger water beetles (Hydrophilidae) *Cryptopleurum minutum* and *Megasternum boletophagum* (Hansen 1987). The silken fungus beetles (Cryptophagidae) and mould beetles (Lathridiidae) are indicators of drier rotting material such as haystack refuse and stabling materials (Koch 1989b).

Possible indicators of the wider environment outside the enclosure system are also present in some abundance and include grassland and meadow/pasture species and taxa associated with drier meadows and damp, floodplain-type grassland. The ground beetle, *Trechus quadristriatus*, the click beetle (Elateridae), *Athous* spp. and *Agriotes* spp., are found in drier conditions with light vegetation cover. The ground beetle, *T. quadristriatus*, and the seed weevil, *Apion* spp., are particularly associated with docks and sorrels. The pea and bean weevil, *Sitona* spp., feeds upon vetches (*Vicia* spp.) and clover (*Trifolium* spp.) (Koch 1992; Lindroth 1974; 1985; 1986). Both *Apion* spp. and *Sitona* spp. feed on herbaceous taxa characteristic of pasture but are found in greater quantities in hay meadows (Robinson 1981). This part of the assemblage therefore indicates the presence of plants such as clover and vetches which are typical of a grazed sward. Species of wetter grassland and muddy, disturbed ground are less abundant, and include the minute fungus beetle (orthoperid) *Corylophous cassidoides* found in wet tussocky grassland. The ground beetles *Bembidion guttula* and *Pterostichus anthracinus* are strongly associated with damper meadows among sedges (*Carex* spp.) and grasses, particularly in mud around bodies of water (Lindroth 1974; 1985; Robinson 1981).

Several species, found in much smaller numbers, are found in distinctive environments. This includes the ground beetle *Loricera pilicornis* and the click beetle (Elaterid), *Adelocera murina* which are found in shaded ground at the margins of woodland or in hedgerows (Koch 1989a; Lindroth 1974; 1986). Two species are also associated with coastal environments. The ecological preferences of the halobiontic carabid *Amara convexiscula* have been previously discussed, a further species, the weevil (curculionid) *Apion limonii*, is found on saltmarshes with sea-lavenders (*Limonium* spp.) (Bullock 1993).

Discussion

The large and diverse assemblage from the well has produced highly detailed information on the immediate and wider environment. The sheer abundance and diversity of beetles, 93 species and 631 individuals, confirms that deposit formation occurred over a considerable period of time. Wells act as natural 'pitfall traps' and will accumulate large assemblages of insects overtime.

The beetles suggested that the immediate environment was used as a holding pen for livestock. The dung beetle fauna is one of the largest assemblages of this family seen by the author, and was found with a large group of species associated with foul rotting material, such as dung. Certain beetles associated with drier, less foul, rotting organic material have been defined by Kenward and Hall (1995) as 'house' fauna. Although several species from this group were recovered at Rudgeway Lane, the assemblage is too limited to directly suggest waste material associated with human occupation. The source of the house fauna is likely to be a hayrick or similar store of hay or straw used as fodder or stabling material. Animal feed such as hay would provide a source for the meadow and pasture-land species recovered from this sample. Robinson (1981) has suggested that seed, pea and bean weevils (*Apion* and *Sitona* families) are commonly found in pasture but are more abundant in hay meadows. This is not surprising, as on grazed land the herbaceous species have little opportunity to realise their full potential as fresh growth will be quickly eaten. Hay meadows on the other hand allow the plants to grow unchecked until mowing, hence a more abundant and diverse fauna of insects is able to exploit this niche.

A further possible source for these grassland species is the presence of herbaceous species within the enclosure providing additional beetle habitats. This is possible as families such as vetches, clovers and particularly docks and sorrels all include stress-tolerant species, which will exploit this type of disturbed environment. Imported hay is another likely consideration for taxa normally associated with wet grassland and coastal communities.

The wider landscape

The woodland, hedgerow and wetland taxa are likely to have arrived via similar means, possibly from close to the enclosure. Hedges were as common a method of enclosure during the Roman period as they were during later periods of British history and are recorded across the Empire (Rackham 1986). Beetles from these habitats could have been transported by the animals, in their gut or on their coats, or by human agency in fodder brought from external sources.

The small wetland component also perhaps reflects the proximity of the site to the confluence of the River Severn and the River Avon, only 3.5km distant, and more locally the floodplains of the River Swilgate and Tirle Brook. Floodplain grasslands are generally lush, verdant swards of premium grazing land. Evidence of floodplain grazing from the Bronze Age through to the Roman period is well documented in the Thames Valley (e.g. Robinson 1981; 1993a; 1993b; Tetlow 2006a). It seems likely that the floodplain of the River Severn at Tewkesbury would have been exploited in a similar manner.

Conclusions

The insect remains from the well clearly indicate a prolonged episode of deposit accumulation and reflect the environments of the immediate vicinity as well as the conditions in the wider landscape. It is probable that the fauna derive from a range of different vectors. The insect remains suggested that during the Roman period this enclosure was being used either as a stockyard or a holding area for large herbivores, with abundant dung beetles recorded. The insects suggest disturbed, weedy, grass/pastureland environments and may indicate that fodder, in the form of hay, was being imported into the site from salt pastures or water meadows. It is also possible that the animals folded at this site were being grazed on local floodplains.

Radiocarbon dating, by Sylvia Warman

A programme of radiocarbon dating was undertaken to assist with the reconstruction of the site chronology. In order to refine the dating of Period 1 two pot sherds with burnt residues from the fills of Ditch 1, a pot sherd with a residue and a red deer antler fragment from Ditch 5413 were submitted for dating. Human bone from Burial 2 was also selected as this was part of a group of otherwise undated burials. The samples were processed during 2007 at the University of Waikato Radiocarbon Dating Laboratory, Hamilton, New Zealand. For details of the methods and equipment used see University of Waikato 2006.

Results and calibration

The results are conventional radiocarbon ages (Stuiver and Polach 1977) and simple calibrations of the results are given in Table 13. The results were calculated using the calibration curve of Reimer *et al.* (2004) and the computer program OxCal 3.10 (Bronk Ramsey 2005). Date ranges cited in the text are those at 95% confidence level unless otherwise specified. Ranges are derived from the probability method (Stuiver and Reimer 1993).

The antler sample was rejected after pre-treatment due to lack of nitrogen, and the pot residue from Ditch 5413 was too small even for the AMS method. The remaining three samples were successfully dated. The success rate of the samples was slightly disappointing. For most deposits a second option was available, but Ditch 5413 remains undated by absolute means, although it clearly dates to Period 1. The Bronze Age dates for the two pottery residues from separate fills of Ditch 1 match well with the ceramic dating of these features. The human femur from Burial 2 provided a Roman date, and by inference the other burials in this group (Burials 3, 4, and 5) also date to this period.

Table 13: Radiocarbon dates

Period	Laboratory No.	Type	Context no.	Description	Material	Radiocarbon Age (BP)	Calibrated date range (at 2∞ 95.4% confidence)
1	Wk-20710	AMS	Ditch 5413 (5288)	Fill of ditch	Residue on potsherd		Failed
1	Wk-20709	radiometric	Ditch 5413 (5286)	Fill of ditch	Antler		Failed
1	Wk-20711	AMS	Ditch 1 (5366)	Fill of ditch	Residue on potsherd	3202+/-32	1530–1410 cal. BC
1	Wk-21274	AMS	Ditch 1 (5467)	Fill of ditch	Residue on potsherd	3098+/-34	1440–1260 cal. BC
4b	Wk-21277	radiometric	SK 2 (5869)	Burial 2	Human femur	1882+/-82	50 cal. BC–350 cal. AD

DISCUSSION

Early Prehistoric, by Timothy Darvill

The pair of parallel ditches and associated features in Area A provide a challenge to interpretation as numerous possibilities exist given the recorded ground-plan, the eroded nature of the interior surface, which may have led to the loss of significant and distinctive features, and the relative poverty of dateable material. The primary silts and lowest fills are undated, allowing the possibility that in origin they are rather earlier than the date suggested by the finds and mid 2nd millennium BC radiocarbon date from midway up the sequence of fills (which indeed might have been within a recut). Three possible interpretations are considered plausible, of which the first seems most likely.

First, that these are the quarry ditches of a medium-sized plough-levelled long barrow; the stones in the lower ditch fills being the remains of a central mound. While numerous stone-built long barrows are known on the Cotswold uplands (Darvill 2004) no certain examples are known in the lower Severn Valley or upper Thames Valley and it is unclear what earthen long barrows in these areas might look like. A pair of ditches broadly similar to those at Rudgeway Lane was recognised during excavations at Cleveland Farm, Ashton Keynes, Wiltshire (Powell *et al.* 2008, 23) although they are slightly shorter, at 22m, and rather narrower with a tapering plan some 4m apart at the northwest end and 5.5m apart at the southeast. Much the same was found at Wasperton, Warwickshire (Hughes and Crawford 1995, 9) where the pair of roughly parallel ditches were 15.5m and 13m long respectively and up to 5m apart. At Raunds, Northamptonshire, a pair of parallel ditches each about 20m long and set 10m apart cut into the top of a turf mound and were perhaps quarries for a low linear mound. The feature was dated to 3750–3620 BC (Harding and Healy 2008, 70–3). Larger and more widely spaced parallel ditches are well known among earthen long barrows in Wessex as, for example at South Street, Wiltshire, where the ditches were 43m long and about 28m apart. There was no evidence of a chamber within that barrow and apart from stakeholes representing the lines of hurdlework fences subdividing the barrow mound there were rather few sub-surface features (Ashbee *et al.* 1979, 250–98). Long barrow ditches are often non-symmetrical, as here, and are sometimes recut or their part-silted hollows become repositories for cultural debris in later prehistory.

A second possibility is that these ditches form two edges of a roughly square enclosure, the other two sides being either left open or closed by a light fence or hedge without a flanking ditch. Superficially similar features are known at Gwithian, Cornwall (Megaw 1976, fig. 4.1), although the linear boundaries east and west of the settlement area are probably best considered elements of a fieldsystem.

A third possibility focuses on land boundaries defining units within fieldsystems. At Perry Oaks, Middlesex, for example, short lengths of parallel ditch appear to have formed extensions to more substantial co-axial systems. The land-units were generally 30–40m wide and ditch segments less than 100m in length were fairly common (Framework Archaeology 2006, fig. 3.11). Against this interpretation is the apparent absence of a co-axial fieldsystem in the area and the size of the ditches, which are rather large for the boundaries/drainage ditches of typical prehistoric fieldsystems.

Iron Age and Romano-British, by Neil Holbrook

While the settlement at Rudgeway Lane bears many comparisons with Romano-British Sites I and II on the Eastern Relief Road, it does provide a number of fresh insights into the nature of later Iron Age and Romano-British rural settlement in this part of the Severn Valley. Preservation was better at this site than at the other two, and the recovery of insect fauna and human skeletal remains provides evidence not encountered there.

The earliest activity detectable in Area D was the construction in Period 2 of a small ditched enclosure, *c.* 25m long by 20m wide, with a south-east facing entrance (Enclosure 1; Fig. 20). No evidence of any internal features was found. The small quantities of pottery recovered from the ditch are consistent with occupation at some point within the period from the 4th to 2nd century BC. This small enclosure invites comparison with similar-sized rectilinear examples at Beckford II and Evesham in Worcestershire, the latter also dating to the Middle Iron Age (Edwards and Hurst 2000; Moore 2006, 91–2). At these sites the enclosures appear to be one element within larger polyfocal unenclosed settlements, and this may also have been the case here, although no other Middle Iron Age features were found in the excavated areas. However it should be borne in mind that mass-built houses which did not possess drip gullies can be virtually invisible to detect through geophysical survey or indeed excavation (Holbrook 2003, 63).

There can be no certainty whether Enclosure 1 was abandoned long before the start of Period 3, or whether Periods 2 and 3 were more or less continuous. The absence of any evidence for recutting of the ditch suggests that occupation within Enclosure 1 was not protracted, and in the absence of evidence to the contrary, it is simplest to favour continuity over discontinuity. This certainly seems to be the case at Frocester where a ditched enclosure which originated in the Middle Iron Age dictated the form of all subsequent occupation on the site until the construction of a Roman villa in the late 3rd century AD (Price 2000). If continuity is represented at Rudgeway Lane we can envisage that Enclosure 1 continued in use until the 1st century AD when a new layout was adopted. This Period 3 settlement comprised an ovoid ditched enclosure 8–12m in diameter which presumably surrounded a roundhouse (Enclosure 3). Geophysical survey to the south of Enclosure 3 detected three or four curvilinear anomalies of similar size to Enclosure 3 (see Fig. 6, A, B, C, D). They most probably mark the locations of other houses, and sampling of the enclosures by evaluation trenching produced pottery consistent with that found in Period 3 features. To the north, Ring ditch 1 presumably defines the site of another roundhouse of this period, while to the west of Enclosure 3 there was an agricultural enclosure or paddock. This was defined on its west side by a north-south ditch which had a gap within it. Presumably differing land uses took place on either side of this ditch, perhaps open pasture to the west on the highest part of the ridge and stock raising and settlement to the east. The absence of a contemporary enclosing ditch, either within the excavation area or on the geophysical survey, demonstrates that the Period 3 settlement was, like that of Period 2, essentially unenclosed. Moore (2006, 93–7) has drawn attention to the presence on later Iron Age unenclosed settlements in the Cotswold-Severn region of roundhouses contained within individual enclosures, including examples at Abbeymeads and Saintbridge near Gloucester. Enclosure 3 at Rudgeway Lane can now be added to these examples.

In the 2nd century AD the unenclosed settlement was replaced by a large rectilinear ditched enclosure with an associated trackway to the south. Tellingly the trackway was

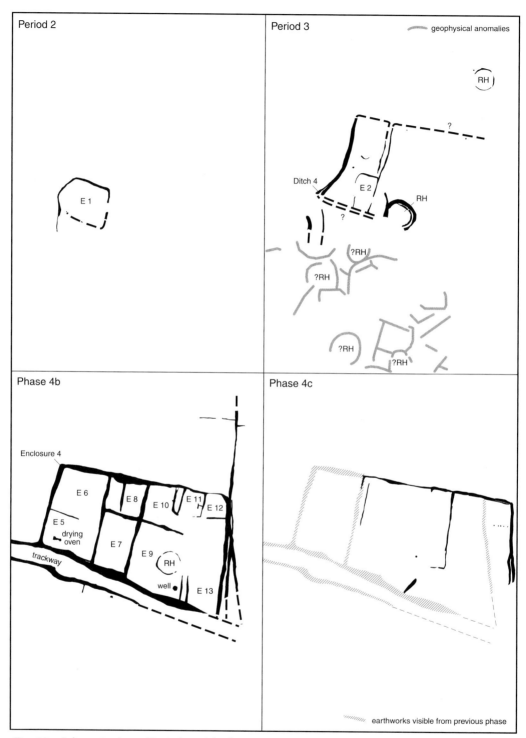

Fig. 20: Schematic plans of Periods 2–4 (scale 1:2000)

aligned on the gap within the Period 3 boundary ditch and it presumably represents the formularisation of a pre-existing unditched droveway. This observation demonstrates a strong element of settlement continuity between Periods 3 and 4 and comparison might be made with sites in the Upper Thames Valley such as Gravelly Guy, Oxfordshire, where an unenclosed Early-Middle Iron Age settlement was laid out in relation to a linear boundary parallel with the river Windrush. This settlement was abandoned in the late Iron Age and early Roman period when it was replaced by a series of paddocks, enclosures and domestic occupation aligned on the pre-existing boundary (Lambrick and Allen 2004). In terms of size and morphology Enclosure 4 invites comparison with similar enclosures at Romano-British Sites I and II on the Eastern Relief Road and at Brockworth near Gloucester (Fig. 21). This was by no means the only layout adopted by Romano-British farmsteads in this part of the Severn Valley, however, as the trapezoidal enclosure at Frocester and the curvilinear stock enclosure and associated rectangular building at Ripple, Worcestershire highlight (Price 2000; Barber and Watts 2008).

In all cases we can be confident that the enclosures functioned as farms, although it can be difficult to discern the precise modes of agricultural production. At Rudgeway Lane Enclosure 4 was divided into a number of sub-enclosures, presumably to separate activities such as the breeding and folding of stock, storage and processing of crops (testified by the drying oven in sub-Enclosure 5) and habitation (sub-Enclosure 9). The environmental evidence from the well indicates the proximity of pasture and meadow, and there are indications that hay was brought into the enclosure from salt pastures or water meadows for fodder. The absence of mature cattle in the animal bone assemblage suggests that cattle were raised on the farm and then taken off site for slaughter. The same may be true for sheep/goat, although conceivably the mature species were kept on the farm for wool and milk rather than meat. The geophysical survey shows that the trackway only extended for a distance of c.15m to the west of Enclosure 4, and this was therefore only required to control the movement of stock within the vicinity of the settlement. As in Period 3 we may envisage open pasture on the slightly higher land to the west and that stock was brought down in the summer months to feed on the lush grassland bordering the Tirle Brook to the east of the enclosure. While the insect fauna from the well provides little evidence for arable cultivation, the drying oven does testify to the growing of crops, presumably wheat and barley, and these fields may have lain to the south of the trackway. The ridge and furrow which covers the low ridge between the Swilgate and the Tirle Brook plainly demonstrates that this area was good arable land in the medieval period, and there is no reason to believe that it was any different in the Roman period. Unfortunately the poor preservation of plant remains makes it difficult to assess the contribution of crops to the agricultural economy of the farmstead, although we may also note that only three fragments of quern stone were recovered, which would support the other evidence that pastoralism rather than arable was the dominant activity here. Drying ovens such as that in sub-Enclosure 5 were multi-functional, possible activities including the drying of grain in preparation for consumption and storage, or the roasting of germinated grains of barley for the production of malt for use in brewing (Van der Veen 1989).

The enclosure continued in use until at least until the late 3rd century AD, but most of the main enclosure ditches had largely silted up by the 4th century. Some recutting occurred in Phase 4c but activity appears to have been on a much reduced scale compared to that in the 2nd and 3rd centuries. The latest firmly dated Roman artefact recovered from the site is the coin of AD 330–5 from the hollow above the abandoned drying oven, and

71

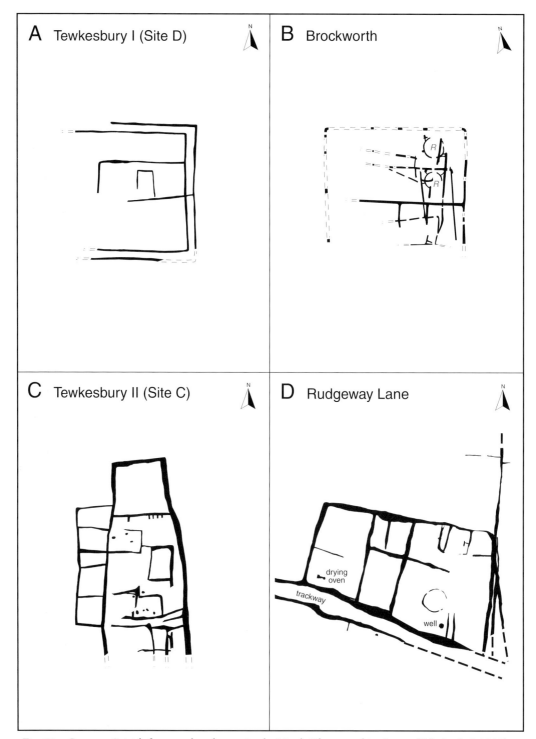

Fig. 21: Romano-British farmstead enclosures in the North Gloucestershire Severn Vale (scale 1:2000)

the absence of other Constantinian and later coins from the site suggests that most activity had ceased by the early-mid 4th century.

We can therefore reconstruct the chronological sequence at Site D as follows. An essentially unenclosed rural settlement, of which Enclosure 1 was but one constituent, was most probably established around the 2nd century BC. Whether occupation was continuous or not is unclear, but by the 1st century AD Enclosure 1 had been abandoned and the site occupied by several roundhouses, some set within individual ditched enclosures. Sometime in the 2nd century the unenclosed roundhouses were replaced by a large rectilinear enclosure which continued in use until at least the late 3rd century. By the 4th century, however, the ditches had largely silted up although activity persisted on the site for some decades.

It is now worth examining how the Rudgeway Lane sequence compares with those recovered on other farmstead sites in the region. Eastern Relief Road Site II was established in the Late Iron Age or early Roman period and continued in use until the first half of the 4th century, while occupation at Site I was restricted to the 2nd to early 3rd centuries. In both cases it would appear that the rectilinear ditched enclosures were later additions to initially unenclosed settlements (Walker *et al.* 2004). At Brockworth the enclosure was established in the second half of the 1st century AD and was occupied into the later 4th century at least (Rawes 1981), while occupation at nearby Hucclecote started in the 1st century AD and ended in the earlier 4th century when the focus of activity may have shifted to a villa house 650m distant (Thomas *et al.* 2003). To the north of Tewkesbury, the farmstead at Ripple was established during the early 2nd century AD but had been abandoned by the early 3rd century at latest (Barber and Watts 2008). In the valley of the Carrant Brook and River Isbourne four sites were sampled during the construction of gas pipeline (Coleman *et al.* 2006). In two cases Middle or Late Iron Age enclosures continued in use until the end of the 1st century AD when they were abandoned, while at the other two sites activity started, or recommenced after a gap, in the 2nd century AD. All four sites were abandoned during the 3rd or 4th centuries.

While no common chronology applies to all these farmsteads, some trends are discernible. Continuity of occupation on Iron Age sites into the Roman period is evident, although some of these sites were abandoned in the late 1st or 2nd centuries AD. Around the same time other sites were established for the first time at new locations. The 2nd and 3rd centuries seem to represent the highpoint in activity, with abandonment or reduced occupation the norm in the 4th century. It would be too simplistic to interpret these sequences as evidence of declining agricultural production in the 4th century, however, and in order to gain a more reliable picture we need to examine a broader range of evidence. Reclamation of the saltmarshes along the east bank of the river Severn to the south of Gloucester in the later Roman period, and the development of villas in the Vale around the same time, both point to the vitality of the rural economy (Holbrook 2006, 119). Intensification of agricultural production perhaps rendered the small farmsteads uneconomic, and larger estates, some centred on villa houses, may have become increasingly prevalent. Probable villas are known at Southwick Park, Tewkesbury Park, and perhaps Deerhurst within a 4km radius of Rudgeway Lane, and others probably await discovery (Marshall 1976, 30; Rawes 1973; Rahtz and Watts 1997, 154–6). Rather than being the cause of agricultural intensification, it is more likely that villa houses, as manifestations of wealth, were a consequence of developments in agricultural practice and land tenure in the 3rd century. Nor should we exclude the effect that the growth of a small town or market centre at Tewkesbury (if that is what it actually was) might have had on settlement pattern of its immediate hinterland. We know little about the form or chronology of Roman Tewkesbury, but by analogy with other small towns in south-west Britain, the peak of activity probably occurred there in the later Roman period. Perhaps the land between the Swilgate and Tirle Brook was directly farmed by workers living in Tewkesbury in the 4th century?

Another aspect of the excavated data worthy of some further discussion is the evidence for superstition and ritual. The deposition of inhumation burials in scattered graves, ditches and other features is now recognised as a commonplace occurrence at Roman rural establishments, and in some ways the absence of such burials at Sites I and II on the Eastern Relief Road is more unusual than their presence here. The symbolism and beliefs associated with this practice are unclear although it would be wrong to believe that their scattered locations necessarily indicate a lack of care or respect for the individuals (Pearce 1999). The burials date to Periods 3 and 4b and most were laid out in the flexed posture typical of the later Iron Age and early Roman tradition of inhumation burial known in the Gloucestershire Severn Vale (Holbrook 2006, 12; Moore 2006, 110–4). The burial evidence should be considered as but one part of a wider pattern of ritual behaviour and structured deposition evidenced in deposits at this site. A neonatal human burial and pottery vessel were interred at the bottom of ovoid Enclosure 3 surrounding a Period 3 roundhouse. At the base of Period 4a ditch 6637 the complete rim of a Severn valley ware vessel and an almost complete jar were placed (or concealed?) beneath a dump of redeposited natural clay. The best evidence for ritual activity, however, derives from the well adjacent to the roundhouse in sub-enclosure 9. The primary silt within the well evidently accumulated over a period of time, to judge from the insect fauna contained within it. However, the silt also contained six substantially complete narrowed-rimmed jars and a costrel. The special nature of this deposit is emphasised by the costrel, a form which is not otherwise represented in Severn Valley ware in the myriad of published site assemblages from the region. The silts also contained a large quantity of animal bones, including the larger parts of two sheep and three foxes which must have been deposited rapidly with flesh still attached, along with an iron hook. On the interface of the silts and the overlying backfill of the well lay the body of a young adult male whose skeleton showed evidence of an infection such as pneumonia or tuberculosis, although this illness was receding at the time of death.

The prevalence of unusual deposits of artefacts and ecofacts in Romano-British pits, especially wells, has been remarked upon by Fulford (2001). Complete or near complete ceramic vessels are relatively commonplace finds amongst the wells excavated at Silchester, Hampshire, and they were often accompanied by whole, or partially articulated, animals of various sorts and sometimes disarticulated fragments of human bone. Another probable structured deposit has recently been published from a non-villa farmstead at Yeovilton in south Somerset where a well yielded six dogs, a cat, a domestic fowl, an abundance of sheep bones and two almost complete pottery vessels (Lovell 2006, 17, 36, 44–7). The presence of a human skeleton within the well at Rudgeway Lane can be regarded as another manifestation of the disposal of the dead in various localities within the settlement remarked upon above, and indeed a continuation of the Iron Age tradition of human burial within pits. Two other comparable examples of the burial of human bodies in wells can be cited from Roman villas in south-west England. At Brislington, Bristol, a well, filled sometime after AD 337, contained the skeletal remains of four or five individuals along with a dozen cattle (Branigan 1972). At North Wraxall, Wiltshire, three skeletons were found in the well accompanied by fragments of column shaft (Scrope 1862). In the light of the evidence collected by Fulford it seems more likely that at both sites we should consider the assemblages as structured 'closure' deposits associated with the ritual sealing of the wells rather than as evidence for the sacking of the villas in the Barbarian Conspiracy in AD 367 (Branigan 1976, 93–6). The recognition of ritual activity is therefore significant at Rudgeway Lane, even if we cannot at present understand much of the meaning and significance behind the practices that we have begun to identify.

Anglo-Saxon, by Mary Alexander

Burials 8 and 9 were laid side by side, although 6m apart, on a north/south alignment with the head to the south, both possibly interred in coffins. The burials were aligned with the Roman enclosure boundaries and Burial 9 was dug into a silted up ditch. The glass-headed pin from a Roman context 10m to the north has Anglo-Saxon parallels and may represent a disturbed third burial of this period. The five amber and four terracotta-coloured opaque glass beads found with female Burial 9 suggest a date in the 6th or early 7th century. These two burials lay beyond the western limit of 6th and 7th-century Anglo-Saxon cemeteries and burials with Germanic associations (Reynolds 2006, 144), and represent the most westerly of their type in the region.

There are similarities between the Rudgeway Lane burials and those of the closest excavated cemeteries at Beckford, Worcestershire approximately 9.5km to the north-east (Evison and Hill 1996), and Bishop's Cleeve 9km to the south-east (Holbrook 2000). A north/south alignment with the head to the south was used exclusively at Bishop's Cleeve and almost exclusively at Beckford, and burials were frequently accompanied by glass and amber beads. The associated brooches and buckles suggest cultural affinities with the Upper Thames Valley, which is also implied by the buckle from Burial 9 at Rudgeway Lane. The worn condition of the grave goods at Bishop's Cleeve and the limited range of material at Beckford hint at communities with infrequent trade or cultural contact with their source. The population represented at Beckford was remarkably free of degenerative joint disease associated with physical work (Wells 1996), whereas trauma from physical activity was apparent on both individuals at Rudgeway Lane, with the frequent lifting or carrying of heavy loads indicated for the female (Burial 9).

The nearest known evidence for contemporary settlement is located 6km to the north-east of Rudgeway Lane in the valley of the Carrant Brook. This comprises two single sunken-featured buildings c. 1.5km apart at Aston Mill Farm and Kemerton, both accompanied by peripheral features (Dinn and Evans 1990, Fagan et al. 1994). At Bank Farm, Wormington, further east a single burial of a young adult without gravegoods, dated between the early 5th and early 7th centuries by radiocarbon assay was found in a Roman enclosure. A single ditch ascribed to this period and intrusive Anglo-Saxon pottery found in earlier features argues for occupation, as well as burial among earlier earthworks (Coleman et al. 2000, 20). On the east bank of the River Severn at Ryall Quarry, Ripple, Worcestershire, 8km to the north of Rudgeway Lane, seven sunken-featured buildings date to the 6th to 7th centuries (Barber and Watts 2008). Overall the sparse evidence for 5th to 7th-century occupation in the region gives an impression of dispersed, small, and possibly isolated settlements. The location of larger settlements, if present, remains elusive, as is noted throughout the Gloucestershire area (Reynolds 2006). Anglo-Saxon cemeteries and isolated burials of this date are fairly numerous in the Upper Thames Valley and extend north and north-west across the Cotswolds to include the Rudgeway Lane examples. This distribution helps to define the limits of a British territory centred on Gloucester that may not have succumbed to Saxon control until the 7th century (Heighway 1984, 231).

The burials lay close to the edge of the parish boundary between Walton Cardiff and Ashchurch, which runs along the field boundary to the south of the site. The parish of Walton Cardiff gained independent status in the 17th century but was originally the most easterly extent of the parish of Tewkesbury and was part of the manor of Tewkesbury before the Norman Conquest (Elrington 1968, 236–42). In the Late Saxon period Tewkesbury was locally important as an administration centre of a large and wealthy estate for which a church and market is recorded, and may have been a Saxon Minster (Heighway 2003, 5–6). However, there is no archaeological evidence to espouse any Anglo-Saxon origin, and only a single sherd of Late Saxon pottery was associated with the remains of a substantial timber building of medieval or Late Saxon form found at Holm Hill on the south-eastern edge of Tewkesbury. This structure was replaced by a high status building which was probably the remains of the Norman Manor House (Hannan 1993; 1997).

The burials at Rudgeway Lane fall within a period in which reuse of ancient monuments is 'particularly prevalent' (Williams 1997, 3) and it is within this context that these burials must be studied. Almost all types of monument have been reused, ranging from Neolithic barrows through to Roman ritual monuments and including features originally constructed with no apparent spiritual association and, on occasion, natural landscape features of similar appearance (Lucy 2000, 128). This range of sites suggests that the visibility and a collective cultural memory of the significance of these monuments were the overriding factors in the choice of location (ibid., 130). It has been proposed that burial in or adjacent to monuments invested with ancestral and spiritual power helps to maintain ideologies and social order and therefore would be particularly important at times of territorial unrest. This burial practice, in which individual burials and small groups of burials predominate, may have been undertaken by a pre-existing tribal power as easily as a new élite wishing to establish dominance. The Rudgeway Lane burials and perhaps the burial at Bank Farm, Wormington, may reflect this practice if, as is suggested, they are located on a cultural and possibly political frontier between Anglo-Saxon and British territories (Reynolds 2006, 144). The Late Iron Age and Roman features at Rudgeway Lane would still have been visible in the landscape, given that the major components of the Roman fieldsystem were up to 1m in depth when excavated.

Gravegoods denoting wealth and power are often found with isolated burials in this period. The gravegoods found with Burial 9 at Rudgeway Lane do not denote a particularly rich burial, but neither do they suggest 'outcast' status, being consistent with the normal range of material found with 6th-century female burials (Evison 1987). The presence of amber beads may be an indication of higher status, as the evidence at Beckford suggests (Evison and Hill 1996).

An adjunct to this discussion is the relationship between burial sites and boundaries. Both excavated evidence and medieval boundary charters have been used to identify boundary locations as a deliberate choice for pre-Christian burial sites (Arnold and Wardle 1981; Bonney 1966; Lucy and Reynolds 2002) and Reynolds (2009) has argued that there is an even stronger association between Anglo-Saxon burials and routeways. The Rudgeway Lane burials lie within 20m of the parallel ditches of the earlier trackway, and although there is no archaeological evidence to suggest that the track was in use in the 6th century, the alignment is preserved in the field boundary, which formed the parish boundary between Tewkesbury and Ashchurch (see Fig. 2). Although it is tempting to suggest this signifies the preservation of an ancient territorial boundary, its survival is probably the result of a practical re-use of a convenient earthwork as a field ditch, which was later adapted as a parish boundary.

ACKNOWLEDGEMENTS

The excavation and this publication were generously funded by J.S. Bloor Limited. We are grateful to Adrian Bloor of Bloor Homes for his support and assistance. The excavation was managed by Simon Cox and led by Laurent Coleman (Areas A–C) and Jonathan Hart (Area D). Post-excavation was managed by Annette Hancocks, and the illustrations were prepared by Peter Moore, Lorna Gray and Jemma Elliot. The excavations were monitored by Charles Parry, Gloucestershire County Council Archaeology Service, on behalf of Tewkesbury Borough Council. The text was edited by Annette Hancocks and Neil Holbrook. We are grateful to the field team who worked on this site in difficult conditions over the winter months, and the specialists who have contributed to this report. Dr Jeremy Taylor and Neil Holbrook kindly read an earlier version of this report and made a number of helpful comments which have resulted in its improvement. We are also grateful to Timothy Darvill and Carolyn Heighway for their input into the prehistoric and Anglo-Saxon sections respectively. The project archives and finds will be deposited with Cheltenham Museum and Art Gallery under accession numbers CAGM 2002.167 and CAGM 2004.144.

BIBLIOGRAPHY

Allen, T.G. and Robinson, M.A. 1993 *The prehistoric landscape and Iron Age enclosed settlement at Mingies Ditch, Hardwick with Yelford, Oxon* Oxford, Oxford Archaeological Unit

Arnold, C. and Wardle, P. 1981 'Early medieval settlement patterns in England', *Medieval Archaeol.* **25**, 145–9

Ashbee, P., Smith, I.F. and Evans, J.G. 1979 'Excavation of three long barrows near Avebury, Wiltshire', *Proc. Prehist. Soc.* **45**, 207–300

Aufderheide, A.C. and Rodríguez-Martín, C. 1998 *The Cambridge encyclopaedia of human paleopathology* Cambridge, Cambridge University Press

Barber, A. and Watts, M. 2008 'Excavations at Saxon's Lode Farm, Ripple, 2001–2: Iron Age, Romano-British and Anglo-Saxon rural settlement in the Severn valley', *Trans. Worcestershire Archaeol. Soc.* **21**, 1–90

Barker, J., Forcey, C., Jundi, S. and Witcher, R. (eds) 1999 *TRAC 98: proceedings of the eighth annual theoretical Roman archaeology conference, University of Leicester, April 1998* Oxford, Oxbow Books

Behrensmeyer, A.K. 1978 'Taphonomic and ecological information from bone weathering', *Paleobiology* **4 (2)**, 150–62

Boessneck, J. 1969 'Osteological differences between sheep (*Ovis aries* Linne) and Goat (*Capra hircus* Linne)', in Brothwell and Higgs (eds) 1969, 331–58

Bonney, D. 1966 'Pagan Saxon burials and boundaries in Wiltshire', *Wilts. Archaeol. Natur. Hist. Mag.* **61**, 25–30

Boon, G.C. 1966 'Legionary ware at Caerleon?', *Archaeol. Cambrensis* **115**, 45–66

Branigan, K. 1972 'The Romano-British villa at Brislington', *Proc. Somerset Archaeol. Natur. Hist. Soc.* **116**, 78–85

Branigan, K. 1976 *The Roman villa in south-west England* Bradford-on-Avon, Moonraker

Bronk Ramsey, C. 2005 *OxCal version 3.10* http://c14.arch.ox.ac.uk/embed.php?File= oxcal.html (accessed 29 December 2008)

Brothwell, D.R. and Higgs E.S. (eds) 1969 *Science in archaeology* London, Thames and Hudson

Brugmann, B. 2004 *Glass beads from early Anglo-Saxon graves: a study of the provenance and chronology of glass beads from early Anglo-Saxon graves, based on visual examination* Oxford, Oxbow Books

Bryant, V. and Evans, J. 2004a 'Iron Age and Romano-British pottery', in Dalwood and Edwards 2004, 240–80

Bryant, V. and Evans, J. 2004b 'Slab-built vessels', in Dalwood and Edwards 2004, 366

Bullock, J.A. 1993 'Host plants of British beetles: a list of recorded associations', *Amateur Entomologist* **11a**, 1–24

Burgess, C. and Miket, R. (eds) 1976 *Settlement and economy in the third and second millennia BC* BAR British Series **33**, Oxford, British Archaeological Reports

CA (Cotswold Archaeology) 2002 *Land to the east of Rudgeway Lane, Walton Cardiff, Tewkes- bury, Gloucestershire: archaeological evaluation* CA unpublished report no. **02100**

CA (Cotswold Archaeology) 2006 *Land east of Rudgeway Lane, Tewkesbury, Gloucestershire. Post-excavation assessment and updated project design* CA unpublished report no. **06049**

CA (Cotswold Archaeology) 2007 *Wheatpieces phase 2, Tewkesbury, Gloucestershire: arch- aeological watching brief* CA unpublished report no. **07142**

CAT (Cotswold Archaeological Trust) 1991 *Stonehills, Tewkesbury, Gloucestershire: fieldwalking report* CAT unpublished report no. **9158**

CAT (Cotswold Archaeological Trust) 1992 *Land to the south and east of Tewkesbury, Gloucestershire: archaeological evaluation* CAT unpublished report no. **9273**

CAT (Cotswold Archaeological Trust) 1993a *Additional land to the south and east of Tewkesbury, Gloucestershire: fieldwalking survey* CAT unpublished report no. **93114**

CAT (Cotswold Archaeological Trust) 1993b *Additional land to the south and east of Tewkesbury, Gloucestershire: report on the results of an archaeological evaluation* CAT unpublished report no. **93137**

Clanton, T.O. and DeLee, J.C. 1982 'Osteochondritis dissecans: history, pathophysiology and current treatment concepts', *Clinical Orthopedic Rel. Res.* **167**, 50–64

Coleman, L., Hancocks, A. and Watts, M. 2006 *Excavations on the Wormington to Tirley pipeline, 2000: four sites by the Carrant Brook and River Isbourne Gloucestershire and Worcestershire* Cotswold Archaeology Monograph **3**, Cirencester, Cotswold Archaeology

Cool, H.E.M. 1990 'Roman metal hair pins from southern Britain', *Archaeol. J.* **147**, 148–82

Cox, M. and Mays, S. *Human osteology in archaeology and forensic science* London, Greenwich Medical Media

Crummy, N. 2003 'The metalwork', in Thomas *et al.* 2003, 44–8

Dalwood, H. and Edwards, R. 2004 *Excavations at Deansway, Worcester 1988–89: Romano- British small town to medieval city* CBA Research Report **139**, York, Council for British Archaeology

Dandy, D.J. and Edwards, D.J. 1998 *Essential orthopaedics and trauma* London, Churchill Livingstone

Darvill, T. 2004 *Long barrows of the Cotswolds and surrounding areas* Stroud, Tempus

Davis, S. 1987 *The archaeology of animals* London, Batsford

Dickinson, B. 1996 'Potters stamps and signatures', in Miller *et al.* 1986, 186–98

Dinn, J. and Evans, J. 1990 'Aston Mill Farm, Kemerton: excavation of a ring-ditch, Middle Iron Age enclosures and a grubenhaus', *Trans. Worcestershire. Archaeol. Soc.* **12**, 5–66

Dobney, K. 2001 'A place at the table: the role of vertebrate zooarchaeology within a Roman research agenda for Britain', in James and Millett (eds) 2001, 36–45

Dobney, K. and Rielly, K. 1988 'A method for recording archaeological animal bones: the use of diagnostic zones', *Circaea* **5.2**, 79–96

Driesch, A. von den and Boessneck, J. 1974 'Kritische Anmerkungen zur Widerristhohen-berechnung aus Langenmassen vor-und frühgeschichtlicher Tierknochen', *Säugetier-kundliche Mitteilungen* **22**, 325–48

Edwards, R. and Hurst, J.D. 2000 'Iron Age settlement and a medieval and later farmstead: excavation at 93–97 High Street, Evesham', *Trans. Worcestershire. Archaeol. Soc.* 3 Ser **17**, 73–111

Elrington, C.R. 1968 *A history of the county of Gloucester, volume VIII* Victoria history of the counties of England, Oxford University Press

Evans, C.J., Jones, L. and Ellis, P. 2000 *Severn Valley ware production at Newland Hopfields: excavation of a Romano-British kiln site at North End Farm, Great Malvern, Worcestershire in 1992 and 1994* BAR British Series **313**, Oxford, British Archaeological Reports

Evison, V.I. 1987 *Dover: Buckland Anglo-Saxon cemetery* London, Historic Buildings and Monuments Commission for England Archaeological Report **3**

Evison, V.I. and Hill, P. 1996 *Two Anglo-Saxon cemeteries at Beckford, Hereford and Worcester* CBA Research Report **103**, York, Council for British Archaeology

Fagan, l., Hurst, D. and Pearson, E. 1994 *Evaluation at Kemerton WRW, Kemerton* County Archaeological Service, Hereford and Worcester County Council Report **225**, HWCM 20019

Ford, B.A. 2000 'The Artefacts', in Holbrook 2000, 79–85

Framework Archaeology 2006 *Landscape evolution in the middle Thames Valley. Heathrow Terminal 5 excavations volume 1, Perry Oaks* Salisbury and Oxford, Framework Arch-aeology Monograph **1**

France, N.E. and Gobel, B.M. 1985 *The Romano-British temple at Harlow, Essex* West Essex Archaeological Group, Gloucester, Alan Sutton

Frederico, D.J., Lynch, J.K. and Jokl, P. 1990 '*Osteochondritis dissecans* of the knee: a historical review of etiology and treatment', *J. Arthroscopy and Related Surgery* **6.3**, 190–7

Fulford, M.G. 2001 'Links with the past: pervasive "ritual" behaviour in Roman Britain', *Britannia* **32**, 199–218

Gobel, B.M. 1985 'Iron small finds', in France and Gobel (eds) 1985, 95–9

Goodall, I.H. 1980 *Ironwork in medieval Britain: an archaeological study* Unpublished PhD thesis, University of Cardiff

Grant, A. 1982 'The use of tooth wear as a guide to the age of domestic ungulates', in Wilson *et al.* 1982, 91–108

Green, M. 1998 *Animals in Celtic life and myth* London, Routledge

Green, P. and Branch, N. 2006 'Appendix 15: Geoarchaeology', in CA 2006, 82

Grigson, C. 1982 'Sex and age determination of some bones and teeth of domestic cattle: review of the literature', in Wilson *et al.*1982, 7–23

Guido, M. 1999 *The glass beads of Anglo-Saxon England, c. AD 400–700: a preliminary visual classification of the more definitive and diagnostic types* Woodbridge, Boydell and Brewer for Society of Antiquaries of London

Hambleton, E. 2004 'Faunal remains', in Walker *et al.* 2004, 79–83

Hancocks, A. 1999 'The pottery', in Parry 1999, 104–9

Hannan, A. 1993 'Excavations in Tewkesbury 1972–74', *Trans. Bristol Gloucestershire Archaeol. Soc.* **111**, 21–75

Hannan, A. 1997 'Tewkesbury and the earls of Gloucester: Excavations at Holm Hill, 1974–5,' *Trans. Bristol Gloucestershire Archaeol. Soc.* **115**, 79–231

Hansen, M. 1987 *The Hydrophilidae (Coleoptera) of Fennoscandia and Denmark.* Fauna Entomologyca Scandinavica **18**, Leiden, E.J. Brill/Scandinavian Science Press

Harding, D.W. 1974 *The Iron Age in lowland Britain* London, Routledge and Kegan Paul

Harding, J. and Healy, F. 2008 *The Raunds Area Project: A Neolithic and Bronze Age Landscape in Northamptonshire* London, English Heritage

Hawkey, D.E. and Merbs, C.F. 1995 'Activity-induced musculoskeletal stress markers (MSM) and subsistence strategy changes among ancient Hudson Bay Eskimos', *Int. J. Osteoarchaeol.* **5**, 324–8

Heighway, C. 1983 *The east and north gates of Gloucester* Bristol, Western Archaeological Trust Excavation Monograph **4**

Heighway, C. 1984 'Anglo-Saxon Gloucestershire', in Saville (ed.) 1984, 225–47

Heighway, C. 1987 *Anglo-Saxon Gloucestershire* Gloucester, Sutton

Heighway, C. 2003 'Tewkesbury before the Normans' in R.K. Morris and R. Shoesmith (eds) *Tewkesbury Abbey: history, art and architecture* Logaston, Logaston Press, 1–10

Higbee, L. 2006 'The animal bone', in Coleman *et al.* 2006, 67–78

Hilton, R.C., Ball, J. and Benn R.T. 1976 'Vertebral end-plate lesions (Schmorl's nodes) in the dorsolumbar spine', *Ann Rheum. Dis.* **35**, 127–32

Holbrook, N. 2000 'The Anglo-Saxon cemetery at Lower Farm, Bishop's Cleeve: excavations directed by Kenneth Brown 1969', *Trans. Bristol Gloucestershire Archaeol. Soc.* **118**, 61–92

Holbrook, N. 2003 'The discussion', in Thomas *et al.* 2003, 62–7

Holbrook, N. and Bidwell, P.T. 1991 *Roman finds from Exeter* Exeter, Exeter Archaeol. Rep. **4**

Holbrook, N. and Juřica, J. 2006 *Twenty-five years of archaeology in Gloucestershire. a review of new discoveries and new thinking in Gloucestershire, South Gloucestershire and Bristol 1979–2004* Bristol and Gloucestershire Archaeol. Rep. **3**, Cirencester, Cotswold Archaeology

Holbrook, N. 2006 'The Roman period', in N. Holbrook and J. Juřica (eds), 97–131

Hughes, G. and Crawford, G. 1995 'Excavations at Wasperton, Warwickshire, 1980-1985. Introduction and Part 1: the Neolithic and early Bronze Age', *Trans. Birmingham Warwickshire Archaeol. Soc.* **99**, 9–45

Hume, I.N. 1969 *A Guide to artifacts of colonial America* Philadelphia, University of Pennsylvania Press

Hurst, J.D. and Woodiwiss, S. 1992 'Other ceramic objects', in Woodiwiss (ed) 1992, 64

Hylton, T. 1996 'Iron objects', in Williams *et al.* 1996, 120–5

Hylton, T. and Zeepvat, R.J. 1994 'Objects of copper alloy, silver and gold', in Williams and Zeepvat (eds) 1994, 303–21

Ireland, C. 1983 'The Roman pottery', in Heighway 1983, 96–124

Jackson, R. and Napthan, M. 1998 'Interim report on salvage recording of a Neolithic/

Beaker and Bronze Age settlement and landscape at Huntsmans Quarry, Kemerton 1996', *Trans. Worcestershire Archaeol. Soc. 3 ser* **16**, 57–68

James, S. and Millett, M. 2001 *Britons and Romans advancing an archaeological agenda* CBA Research Report **125**, York, Council for British Archaeology

Jessop, L. 1996 *Coleoptera: Scarabaeidae. Handbooks for the Identification of British Insects* **5.11**, Royal Entomological Society of London

Johns, C. 1996 *The jewellery of Roman Britain: Celtic and classical traditions* London, University College Press

Jones, M. and Dimbleby, G. 1981 *The environment of man: the Iron Age to Anglo-Saxon period* BAR British Series **87**, Oxford, British Archaeological Reports

Keely, J. 1986 'The pottery', in McWhirr 1986, 154–89

Kenward, H.K., Hall A.R. and Jones, A.K.G. 1980 'A tested set of techniques for the extraction of plant and animal macrofossils from waterlogged archaeological deposits', *Scientific Archaeol.* **22**, 3–15

Kenward, H.K. and Hall, A.R. 1995 *Biological evidence from Anglo-Scandinavian Deposits at 16–22 Coppergate* Archaeology of York **14/7**, London, Council for British Archaeology

Koch, K. 1989a *Die Käfer Mitteleuropas: Ökologie Band 1* Krefeld, Goecke and Evers Verlag

Koch, K. 1989b *Die Käfer Mitteleuropas: Ökologie Band 2* Krefeld, Goecke and Evers Verlag

Koch, K. 1992 *Die Käfer Mitteleuropas: Ökologie Band 3* Krefeld, Goecke and Evers Verlag

Lambrick, G. and Allen, T. 2004 Gravelly Guy, Stanton Harcourt: the development of a prehistoric and Romano-British community Thames Valley Landscapes **21**, Oxford, Oxford Archaeology

Lindroth, C.H. 1974 *Coleoptera: Carabidae. Handbooks for the identification of British insects* **4.2**, London, Royal Entomological Society

Lindroth, C.H. 1985 *The Carabidae (Coleoptera) of Fennoscandia and Denmark. Fauna Entomologyca Scandinavica* **15**, Part 1 Leiden, E.J. Brill/Scandinavian Science Press

Lindroth, C.H. 1986 *The Carabidae (Coleoptera) of Fennoscandia and Denmark. Fauna Entomologyca Scandinavica* **15**, Part 2, Leiden, E.J. Brill/Scandinavian Science Press

Liversidge, J. 1977 'Roman burials in the Cambridge area', *Proc. Cambridge. Antiq. Soc.* **67**, 11–38

Lovell, J. 2006 'Excavation of a Romano-British farmstead at RNAS Yeovilton', *Proc. Somerset Archaeol. Natur. Hist. Soc.* **149**, 7–70

Lucht, W.H. 1987 *Die Käfer Mitteleuropas* Katalog Krefeld

Lucy, S. 2000 *The Anglo-Saxon way of death* Stroud, Sutton

Lucy, S. and Reynolds, A. (eds) 2002 *Burial in early medieval England and Wales* Society of Medieval Archaeology Monograph **17**, London, Maney

MacGregor, A. and Bolick, E. 1993 *Ashmolean Museum, Oxford: a summary catalogue of the Anglo-Saxon collections (non-ferrous metals)* BAR British Series **230**, Oxford, British Archaeological Reports

MacRobert, E. 1993 'Discussion of the coarse pottery', in Hannan 1993, 62–3

Manning, W.H. 1985 *Catalogue of the Romano-British iron tools, fittings and weapons in the British Museum* London, British Museum Publications

Margary, I.D. 1967 *Roman roads in Britain* London, John Baker

Marney, P.T. 1989 *Roman and Belgic pottery from excavations in Milton Keynes 1972–82* Buckinghamshire Archaeological Society Monograph **2**, Aylesbury, Buckinghamshire Archaeological Society

Marshall, A.J. 1976 'A Romano-British settlement at Southwick Park, Tewkesbury', *Glevensis* **10**, 30

McSloy, E. 2006 'The pottery', in Coleman *et al.* 2006, 37–57

McSloy, E.R., Gilmore, T., Rowe E. and Reynolds A. 2009 'Two Anglo-Saxon Burials at Abbeymeads, Blunsdon St. Andrew, Wiltshire', *Wiltshire Archaeol. Natur. Hist. Mag.* **102**, 160–74

McWhirr, A. 1986 *Houses in Roman Cirencester* Cirencester Excavations **3**, Cirencester, Cirencester Excavation Committee

Megaw, J.V.S, 1976 'Gwithian Cornwall: some notes on the evidence for Neolithic and Bronze Age settlement', in Burgess and Miket (eds) 1976, 51–66

Miller, L., Schofield, J., Rhodes, M. and Dyson, T. 1986 *The Roman Quay at St. Magnus House, London* London Middlesex Archaeol. Soc. Spec. Pap. **8**, London

Moore, T. 2006 *Iron Age societies in the Severn-Cotswolds* BAR British Series **421**, Oxford, British Archaeological Reports

Mudd, A., Williams, R.J. and Lupton, A. 1999 *Excavations alongside Roman Ermin Street, Gloucestershire and Wiltshire: the archaeology of the A419/A417 Swindon to Gloucester road scheme* Oxford, Oxford Archaeological Unit

Myres, J.N.L. 1937 'A prehistoric and Roman site on Mount Farm, Dorchester', *Oxoniensia* **2**, 12–40

Needham, S. 2004 'Bivalve mould and associated material', in Walker *et al.* 2004, 62–6

O'Neil, H. 1967 'Bevan's Quarry round barrow, Temple Guiting, Gloucestershire 1964', *Trans. Bristol Gloucestershire Archaeol. Soc.* **86**, 16–41

Oswald, F. 1936–7 *Index of figure-types on terra sigillata* Liverpool

Parry, C. 1999 'Iron Age, Romano-British and medieval occupation at Bishop's Cleeve: excavations at Gilders Paddock 1989 and 1990–1', *Trans. Bristol Gloucestershire Archaeol. Soc.* **117**, 89–118

Payne, S. 1985 'Morphological distinctions between mandibular teeth of young sheep *Ovis* and goats *Capra*', *J. Archaeol. Sci.*, **12**, 139–47

PCRG (Prehistoric Ceramics Research Group) 1997 *The study of later prehistoric pottery: general policies and guidelines for analysis and publication* PCRG Occas. Pap. 1 and 2

Peacock, D.P.S. 1967 'Romano-British pottery production in the Malvern district of Worcestershire', *Trans. Worcestershire Archaeol. Soc. 3 ser* **1**, 15–28

Peacock, D.P.S. 1968 'A petrological study of certain Iron Age pottery from western England', *Proc. Prehist. Soc.* **34**, 414–26

Pearce, J. 1999 'The dispersed dead: preliminary observations on burial and settlement space in rural Roman Britain', in Barker *et al.* (eds) 1999, 151–62

Pine, J. and Preston, S. 2004 *Iron Age and Roman Settlement and landscape at Totterdown Lane, Horcott near Fairford, Gloucestershire* Thames Valley Archaeological Services Monograph **6**, Reading, Thames Valley Archaeological Services

Powell, A.B., Jones, G.P. and Mepham, L. 2008 'An Iron Age and Romano-British settlement at Cleveland Farm, Ashton Keynes, Wiltshire', *Wiltshire Archaeol. Natur. Hist. Mag.* **101**, 18–50

Price, E.G. 2000 *Frocester. A Romano-British settlement, its antecedents and successors* Stonehouse, Gloucester and District Archaeol. Research Group; 2 vols

Price, J. and Cottam, S. 1998 *Romano-British glass vessels: a handbook* CBA Practical Handbook in Archaeology **14**, York, Council for British Archaeology

Rackham, O. 1986 *The history of the countryside* London, Phoenix Press

Rahtz, P. and Watts, L. 1997 *St. Mary's church, Deerhurst, Gloucestershire: fieldwork, excavations and structural analysis 1971–1984* Woodbridge, Report Research Committee Society Antiquaries London **55**

Rawes, B. 1973 'The Roman site at Tewkesbury Park, *Trans. Bristol Gloucestershire Archaeol. Soc.* **92**, 210–12

Rawes, B. 1981 'The Romano-British site at Brockworth, Gloucestershire', *Britannia* **12**, 45–77

Reimer, P.J., Baillie, M.G.L., Bard, E. *et al.* 2004 'IntCal04 terrestrial radiocarbon age calibration, 0–26 cal kyr BP', *Radiocarbon* **46.3**, 1029–58

Reynolds, A. 2006 'The early medieval period', in Holbrook and Juřica (eds) 2006, 133–60

Reynolds, A. 2009 'Discussion' in McSloy *et al.* 2009

Roberts, C.A. 2002 'The antiquity of leprosy in Britain: the skeletal evidence', in Roberts *et al.* (eds) 2002, 213–22

Roberts, C. and Cox, M. 2003 *Health and disease in Britain from prehistory to the present day* Stroud, Sutton

Roberts, C.A. and Manchester, K. 1995 *The archaeology of disease* Stroud, Sutton

Roberts, C.A., Lewis, M.E. and Manchester, K. (eds) 2002 *The past and present of leprosy: archaeological, historical, palaeopathological and clinical approaches* BAR International Series **1054**, Oxford, British Archaeological Reports

Robinson, M.A. 1981 'The Iron Age to early Saxon environment of the upper Thames terraces', in Jones and Dimbleby (eds) 1981, 251–86

Robinson, M.A. 1993a 'Pre-Iron Age environment and finds' in Allen and Robinson 1993, 7–16

Robinson, M.A. 1993b 'The scientific evidence', in Allen and Robinson 1993, 101–17

Rogers, J. 2001 'The palaeopathology of joint disease', in Cox and Mays (eds) 2001, 163–82

Saville, A. 1984 (ed.) *Archaeology in Gloucestershire* Cheltenham, Cheltenham Art Gallery and Museums and Bristol Gloucestershire Archaeological Society

Scott, I.R. 1999 'Iron objects', in Mudd *et al.* 1999, 390–403

Scrope, G.P. 1862 'On a Roman villa discovered at North Wraxhall', *Wiltshire Archaeol. Natur. Hist. Mag.* **7**, 59–75

Silver, I.A. 1969 'The ageing of domestic animals', in Brothwell and Higgs (eds) 1969, 283–302

Smith, B.H. 1984 'Patterns of molar wear in hunter-gatherers and agriculturalists', *American J. Physical Anthropol.* **63**, 39–56

Spencer, B. 1983 'Limestone tempered pottery from South Wales in the late Iron Age and early Roman period', *Bull. Board Celtic Stud.* **30.3**, 405–19

SSEW (Soil Survey of England and Wales) 1983 *Soils of England and Wales, sheet 5, south-west England* Harpenden

Stace, C. 1991 *New flora of the British Isles* Cambridge, Cambridge University Press

Stickler, T. 2003 'Animal bone', in Thomas *et al.* 2003, 57–60

Stokes, P. and Rowley Conwy, P. 2002 'Iron Age cultigen? Experimental return rates for fat hen (*Chenopodium album* L.)', *Environmental Archaeol.* 7, 95

Stratascan 2001 *Geophysical Survey at Walton Cardiff, Tewkesbury, Gloucestershire* Stratascan typescript report **J1589.2**

Stratascan 2004 *Geophysical Survey Report Walton Cardiff, Tewkesbury, Gloucestershire* Stratascan typescript report **J1865**

Stuiver, M. and Polach, H.A. 1977 'Discussion: reporting of 14C data', *Radiocarbon* **19,** 355–63

Stuiver, M. and Reimer, P.J. 1993 'Extended 14C database and revised CALIB 3.0 14C Age calibration program', *Radiocarbon* **35.1**, 215–30

Terrisse, J. 1968 *Les céramiques sigillées gallo-romaine des Martres-de-Veyre* 19th supplement to Gallia, Paris, Editions du CNRS

Tetlow, E.A. 2006a *The insect remains from Heathrow Terminal 5* Birmingham Archaeo-environmental Rep. **OA-14-06**

Thomas, A., Holbrook, N. and Bateman, C. 2003 *Later prehistoric and Romano-British burial and settlement at Hucclecote, Gloucestershire* Bristol and Gloucestershire Archaeol. Rep. **2**, Cirencester, Cotswold Archaeology

Thompson, I. 1982 *Grog-tempered 'Belgic' pottery of south-eastern England* BAR British Series **108**, Oxford, British Archaeological Reports

Timby, J.R. 2003 'The pottery', in Thomas *et al.* 2003, 31–44

Timby, J.R. 2004a 'Prehistoric pottery', in Walker *et al.* 2004, 59–62

Timby, J.R. 2004b 'Romano-British pottery', in Walker *et al.* 2004, 66–75

Timby, J.R. and Harrison. E. 2004 'Pottery', in Pine and Preston 2004, 55–67

Tingle, M. 2004 'The flint' in Walker *et al.* 2004, 57–9

Tomber, R. and Dore, J. 1998 *The national Roman fabric reference collection: a handbook* London, Museum of London Archaeology Service

University of Waikato Radiocarbon Dating Laboratory 2006 'Operating Procedures' http://www.radiocarbondating.com/operatingproceedures (accessed 17 August 2007)

Van der Veen, M. 1989 'Charred grain assemblages from Roman-period corn driers in Britain', *Archaeol. J.* **146**, 302–19

Walker, G., Thomas, A. and Bateman, C. 2004 'Bronze Age and Romano-British sites south-east of Tewkesbury: evaluations and excavations 1991–7', *Trans. Bristol Gloucestershire Archaeol. Soc.* **122**, 29–94

Webster, P.V. 1976 'Severn Valley ware: a preliminary study', *Trans. Bristol Gloucestershire Archaeol. Soc.* **94**, 18–46

Wells, C. 1996 'Human burials', in Evison and Hill 1996, 41–61

Williams, H. 1997 'Ancient landscapes and the dead: the reuse of prehistoric and Roman monuments in early Anglo-Saxon burial sites', *Medieval Archaeol.* **41**, 1–32

Williams, R.J. and Zeepvat, R.J. 1994 *Bancroft: a late Bronze Age/Iron Age settlement, Roman villa and temple mausoleum vol. 2: finds and environmental evidence* Aylesbury, Buckinghamshire Archaeol. Soc. Monograph **7**

Williams, R.J., Hart, P.J. and Williams, A.T.L. 1996 *Wavendon Gate: a late Iron Age and Roman settlement in Milton Keynes* Aylesbury, Buckinghamshire Archaeol. Soc. Monograph **10**

Willis, S. 1998 'Samian pottery in Britain: exploring its distribution and archaeological potential', *Archaeol. J.* **155**, 82–133

Wilson, B., Grigson, C. and Payne, S. 1982 *Ageing and sexing animal bones from archaeological sites* BAR British Series **109**, Oxford, British Archaeological Reports

Woodiwiss, S. (ed.) 1992 *Iron Age and Roman salt production and the medieval town of Droitwich* CBA Research Report **81**, York, Council for British Archaeology

Woodward, A. 1998 'The pottery', in Jackson and Napthan 1998, 63–5

Young, C.J. 1977 *Oxfordshire Roman pottery* BAR British Series **43**, Oxford, British Archaeological Reports

ROMANO-BRITISH AGRICULTURE AT THE FORMER ST JAMES'S RAILWAY STATION, CHELTENHAM: EXCAVATIONS IN 2000–2001

by Laurent Coleman and Martin Watts

with contributions by
E. Hutchens, L. Loe, E.R. McSloy and S. Warman

INTRODUCTION

Between October 1999 and March 2002 Cotswold Archaeology (CA; then Cotswold Arch-aeological Trust) carried out a programme of archaeological fieldwork on behalf of the John Lewis Partnership at St. James's Car Park, Cheltenham (SO 943 226; Fig. 1). The car park occupied the site of the former St James's railway station. The work was conducted prior to, and during, the construction of a new Waitrose supermarket and associated infrastructure works.

The first stage of archaeological work on the site comprised a desk-based assessment (Wain 1997). This indicated that the site had potential for the survival of prehistoric and Romano-British archaeological remains beneath deposits imported to level the area during railway construction in the 19th century (Rawes 1974, 22). Accordingly Cheltenham Borough Council required that an archaeological evaluation be undertaken prior to the determination of the planning application for the supermarket development. The evaluation established the level of the pre-railway ground surface across the site and found a variety of cut features, including a ditch which contained a single sherd of Romano-British pottery (Coleman 1999, 10–11). The ditch lay in the northern part of the car park at a comparatively shallow depth below the present ground level whereas over the rest of the site the natural was much more deeply buried and no archaeological features were observed. Planning permission was subsequently granted for the development with a condition requiring excavation of an area of c. 4550m^2 at the northern part of the site and a watching brief elsewhere. The excavation was conducted during December 2000 and January 2001 while the watching brief continued intermittently to March 2002 (Fig. 2). An interim report on the excavation was published in 2001 (Coleman and Watts 2001).

The flat surface of St James's car park masked the pre-Victorian topography. The results of the evaluation suggested that in the northern part of the car park there was a relatively flat terrace of Cheltenham Sand (BGS 1988), the southern edge of which appeared to have been cut away by the quarrying of sand or clay. The original ground surface must have sloped down to the south into the valley occupied by the River Chelt, the present course of which lies 150m to the south. Construction of the railway and associated coal yard and sidings led to the importation of bulk deposits to infill the sand pits and level the natural valley.

Archaeological and historical background

Comparatively little is known of the pre-Regency archaeology of this part of Cheltenham (Rawes 1974). A possible Neolithic portal dolmen may once have stood on or near to the site of St James's Station, although there is some uncertainty as to its precise location

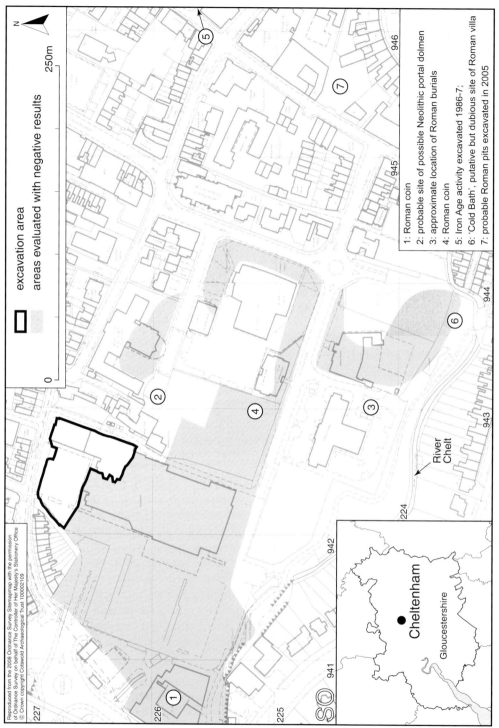

Fig. 1: Location of the excavations and adjacent archaeological discoveries (scale 1:3000)

excavation area

areas evaluated with negative results

0   250m

N

1: Roman coin
2: probable site of possible Neolithic portal dolmen
3: approximate location of Roman burials
4: Roman coin
5: Iron Age activity excavated 1986-7;
6: 'Cold Bath'; putative but dubious site of Roman villa
7: probable Roman pits excavated in 2005

Reproduced from the 2008 Ordnance Survey Sitemapmap with the permission
of Ordnance Survey on behalf of The Controller of Her Majesty's Stationery Office
© Crown copyright Cotswold Archaeological Trust 100002109

River
Chelt

Cheltenham

Gloucestershire

SO

Fig: 2:   View of the northern part of the site during excavation looking north-east

(Rawes 1974, 19–20). The location plotted on Fig. 1 (no. 2) is after Wain 1997, which is in turn based upon the apparent location of the monument shown in a painting of 1830 (reproduced in Darvill 2004, fig. 20). Evaluation immediately to the north of this area in 2001 revealed natural sand at a depth of 1.6–2m below present ground level, sealed by a thick deposit of cultivation soil above which 19th-century walls were found (CAT 2001). Later prehistoric activity in the centre of Cheltenham was confirmed by an excavation in 1986–7 which revealed Iron Age features (Wills 1987, 243–4; Fig. 1, no. 5). Evidence for a Roman cemetery seems to have been uncovered in the area between the railway station and the Chelt in about 1820 when workmen found 'long chests' containing bones, glass bottles, vases and coins. The precise location of these discoveries cannot be accurately determined (the location marked as Fig. 1 no. 3 is that contained in the Gloucestershire SMR). Stone coffins were also found in the adjoining property and on the other side of the Chelt. A number of lead coffins were apparently sold to a local plumber for scrap (Rawes 1974, 20). The site of a reputed Roman villa known as 'Cold Bath' lies to the south-east of the excavation area (Fig. 1, no. 6). John Goding, a local antiquarian, said it comprised walls, hypocausts and mosaics and he dug up there 'many coins, bath tiles, tessellated pavement and portions of pottery' (Goding 1863, 16). The veracity of Golding's account is open to considerable doubt, and interpretation of this site as a Roman villa should be treated with the greatest caution (Rawes 1974, 20). More recently small-scale evaluation at St George's Place found four truncated pits, two of which yielded single sherds of Roman pottery and a fragment of *tegula* roof tile. (Fig. 1 no. 7; CA 2005). Sixteen findspots of Roman coins are listed on the Gloucestershire SMR in central Cheltenham (including Fig. 1, nos 1 and 4). They were mostly found by

19th-century building workers around Bayshill, The Knapp, Lansdown and St Paul's Church (Rawes 1974, 21). Further north in Cheltenham at West Drive, bordering Wyman's Brook in the Pittville district of the town, a fieldsystem, trackways and some evidence of occupation dating principally to the 1st to 3rd centuries AD was excavated in 1997–9 (Catchpole 2002).

The earliest recorded reference to Cheltenham dates from AD 808 and indicates the presence of a religious house that dated back to at least AD 773. This is generally considered to lie near the High Street, within the assumed area of medieval settlement (Saville 1981, 8). The spa waters were first exploited from the early 18th century and Cheltenham under went major expansion in the latter part of that century. The St James's area was transformed by the construction of the Great Western Railway Station in 1847. The station was located just to the south of the excavation site, which was occupied by sidings. By 1900 the original station had been demolished and a new station was built further to the east. The second station was closed in 1966 and demolished shortly afterwards.

Methodology

Natural sand was encountered at a depth of between 1 and 2m below the level of the car park. Following the machine removal of overburden features cut into the natural sand were sampled by hand excavation. The excavation was phased into four areas, with spoil from one area being used to backfill an earlier one once investigation there had been completed. The excavation area shown on Fig. 3 was thus never seen in its entirety at any one time. Subsequently a watching brief was conducted during groundworks on an area immediately to the south of the excavation area and another along the northern bank of the Chelt. No archaeological features were found in either area. Following the completion of the excavation an assessment was made of the findings and proposals made for the programme of analysis which has resulted in this publication. It was considered that further analysis of features and finds dating to the medieval, post-medieval and modern periods, which were mainly associated with sand quarrying and construction of the railway yard, was not warranted. Details of these periods can be found in the site archive, along with full reports on the animal bones and environmental samples recovered from the site, and a geoarchaeological investigation.

EXCAVATION RESULTS

The results of the excavation have been divided into four periods as follows:

Period 0: Mesolithic to Bronze Age
Period 1: Roman (mid/late 1st to late 4th century AD)
Period 2: Post-Roman (5th to 8th centuries AD)
Period 3: Medieval and later

Features dating to Period 2 have been further categorised into four sub-phases through a combination of stratigraphic and artefactual evidence.

Period 0: Mesolithic to Bronze Age

Nineteen worked flint artefacts were recovered as residual finds within the fills of Roman and later features. No patterning to the spatial distribution of these finds could be discerned. Ten pieces exhibit characteristics which indicate Mesolithic or (less likely) earlier Neolithic

Fig. 3:   All feature plan (scale 1:700)

dating, one transverse arrowhead dated to the Late Neolithic period (see Fig. 8) and the remaining material is most likely late Neolithic or Bronze Age.

Period 1: Roman (Figs 4–5)

Although four phases have been identified within the Roman period, it is not suggested

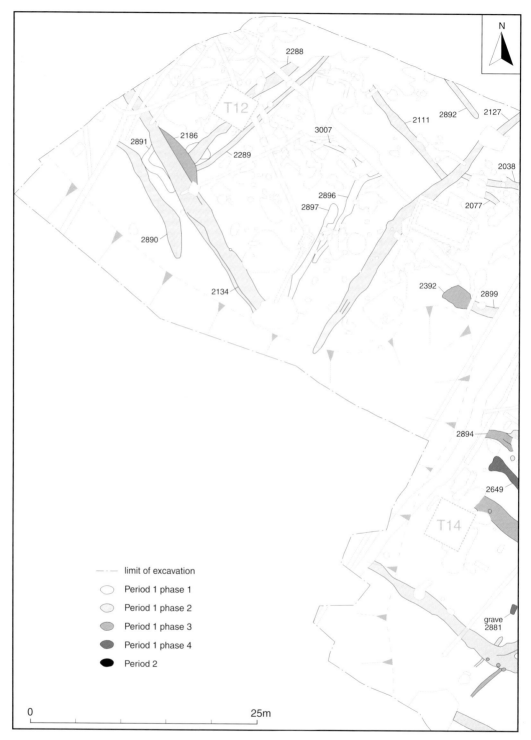

Fig. 4: The western part of the excavation site (scale 1:400)

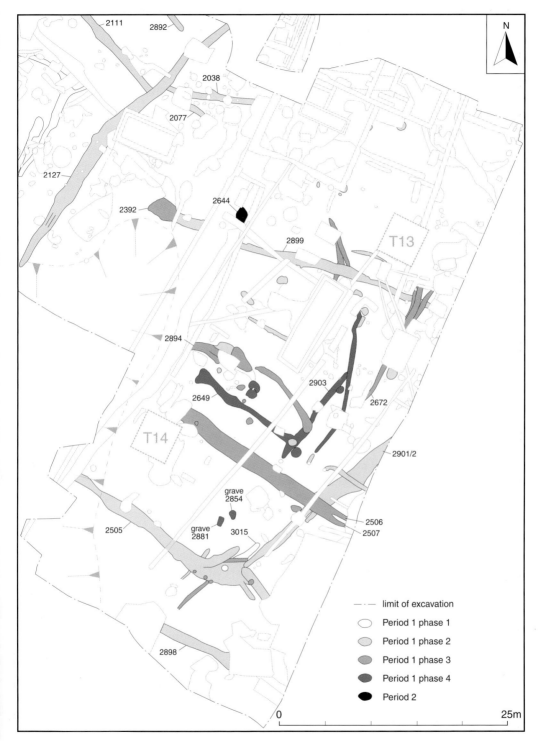

Fig: 5:   The eastern part of the excavation site (scale 1:400)

that there was a hiatus between each phase. Rather four stages within a continuum of activity are envisaged. The fills of the Roman features consistently comprised grey or brown clay silts. Geoarchaeological analysis suggested that these fills did not result from overbank flooding of the Chelt. There must have been frequent cleaning to maintain the boundaries and assist with drainage given the rapidity with which silts accumulated during the course of the excavation.

Phase 1: 1st to 2nd century AD

While the main elements of the fieldsystem were laid out in Phase 2 in the 2nd to 3rd centuries AD, a small number of features pre-dated this event. In the western part of the site ditches 2896 and 2897, up to 1.1m wide and 0.32m deep, were oriented north-east to south-west. To the north and west curving lengths of ditch (2891 and 3007) and three shallow pits were found, and another two small shallow pits and a length of ditch 3015 in the south-east corner of the site.

Phase 2: 2nd to 3rd century AD

A north-east/south-west oriented ditched fieldsystem was established in this phase, with ditches 2127 and 2134 forming major elements within the system. Ditch 2127 ran north-east/south-west and was up to 2.02m wide and 0.66m deep. It may have replaced the Phase 1 ditches 2896 and 2897 further to the north-west. Ditch 2127 drained downslope to the south-west with minor ditches 2111 to the west, and 2038 and 2077 to the east, feeding into it. Ditch 2134 lay at right angles to 2127 and was up to 2.7m wide and 0.72m deep. Both of these major ditches were truncated by post-medieval or modern sand quarrying. The area bounded by these ditches was sub-divided by ditches 2288, 2289, 2892 and 2111. To the east of 2127 the pattern of sub-division is less clear and is represented by a series of heavily truncated north-west/south-east orientated ditches (2899, 2505, 2898). Ditch 2898 contained a complete cow's skull and chaff from the early stages of crop processing. A north-east/south-west oriented pair of intercutting ditches 2901/2902 may form a corner with 2505. Seventeen small pits and postholes were found across the eastern part of the site and were probably contemporary with the Phase 2 ditches. One of these pits was 2.2m in diameter and 0.3m deep, however the remainder were much smaller.

Phase 3: late 3rd to 4th century AD

The field system was subject to continual development into the 3rd to 4th centuries AD with a number of ditches being recut and new ditches added within the existing system. Ditch 2134 was recut by 2186 along part of its length and a large pit 2392 (3.8m long, 2.5m wide and 0.19m deep) dug in the centre of the site. The majority of the features dating to this phase, however, lay within the eastern part of the site. A pair of intercutting ditches 2506 and 2507 aligned north-west/south-east, the latter cutting the former, might have formed a continuation of 2134. An environmental sample recovered from the secondary fill of 2507 produced a mollusc assemblage largely indicative of calcareous, moist, shaded habitats, such as woodland, or perhaps a locally shady area. A number of heavily truncated curvilinear gullies were identified to the north-east of these ditches. Part of the lower stone from a rotary quern was recovered from 2894 and the complete skull of a cow from 2672. Four pits and nine postholes in the eastern part of the site are assigned to this phase, although no structures could be identified from their plan.

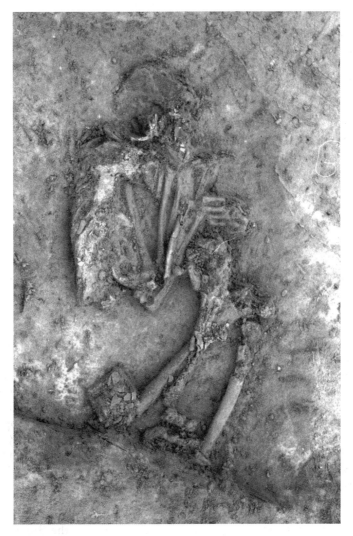

Fig: 6:   Grave 2881

Phase 4: mid to late 4th century AD

Two shallow, amorphous graves aligned north-east/south-west and north/south were dug adjacent to the intersection of a number of field ditches in the south-eastern corner of the site. Grave 2881 was 1.1m long, 0.4–0.6m wide and survived up to 0.15m deep (Fig. 6). It contained the fragmentary skeletal remains of a possible female between 25 and 35 years of age lying in a crouched position on its left side, along with three carpal bones of a young child and a large sherd of pottery datable only to the Roman period. Grave 2854 was 1.15m long, 0.4–0.75m wide and 0.13m deep. It contained only one (unidentifiable) fragment of human bone and a sherd of pottery dating to the late 4th century AD. The graves are assumed to be contemporary and are typical of the scattered burials commonly associated with Romano-British rural settlements. A number of small ditches lay to the north of the graves, one of which (2649) contained the partial skeletal remains of a dog. Two large intercutting pits, two small pits and a posthole were found in the vicinity of these ditches.

Period 2: Post-Roman

An oval pit 2644, 1.6m long, 1.1m wide and 0.35m deep produced a single sherd of hand-made organic tempered pottery broadly datable to the 5th to 8th centuries AD together with Midlands shell-tempered and greyware pottery dating to the late 4th century AD.

Period 3: medieval and later features

Full details on features dating to these periods are contained in the archive. In summary, activity dating to the medieval period was only attested by the recovery of sherds of this date, together with Romano-British sherds, from a post-medieval quarry pit. Post-medieval activity comprised a number of small sub-rectangular and circular pits identified at the northern part of the excavation area. Many of these contained pottery and clay pipes dating to the 17th and/or 18th centuries and may have been dug for small-scale extraction of Cheltenham Sand. Two of these pits had later been used to bury the carcasses of a cow and a pig. Modern activity was characterised by larger pits filled with domestic refuse, the foundations of buildings fronting New Street, and services, structures and levelling dumps associated with the railway.

THE FINDS

Pottery, by E.R. McSloy

Analysis of pottery was restricted to material of Roman date (482 sherds weighing 11.8kg) and the single sherd of post-Roman or Anglo-Saxon type. Preservation of the pottery is generally good, with average sherd weight high at 24g. A number of vessels are preserved to full profile or beyond shoulder level. Surface preservation of the dominant Severn Valley ware fabric is, however, poor. The assemblage was sorted into fabrics macroscopically and quantification is according to sherd count, weight, estimated vessel number (sherd families) and rim EVEs. Recording methodology is compatible with the only other sizeable group of Roman pottery published from Cheltenham (Timby 2002, 92–6). The fabric coding follows Timby's scheme, reflecting National Roman Fabric Reference Codes (Tomber and Dore 1998) and where appropriate type fabric codes.

Assemblage composition

The Roman assemblage spans the entire period from the mid/late 1st century AD to the late 4th/early 5th centuries AD. Quantities of the earliest material are however small and the bulk of the pottery dates to the later 2nd/earlier 3rd and 4th centuries AD (Tables 1–2).

The assemblage is dominated by jars, mainly Severn Valley or Dorset Black-burnished types, which account for 46% of identified forms (by minimum vessel count), and

Table 1: Quantification of the Roman pottery by fabric

Description	Code	Glos. equiv.	Count	Weight (g)	Est. vess.	Rim EVEs
Central Gaulish samian	LEZ SA2	TF8	9	192	8	–
Baetican (Dressel 20 type)	BAT AM1	TF10	1	34	1	–
Savernake ware	SAV GT	TF6	10	364	1	.10
Grog tempered	LOC GT	TF2a	20	143	13	.07
Black sandy (north Wilts?)	LOC BS	–	6	85	6	.10
Miscellaneous grey	LOC GW	–	16	168	16	–
Fine flagon fabric, cream slip	OX CS	–	13	171	1	.50
Miscellaneous oxidised	LOC OX	–	5	51	5	–
Severn valley ware early variants	SVW ET	TF17	31	430	17	.55
Severn Valley ware oxidised	SVW OX	TF11B	222	7297	195	3.88
Severn Valley ware reduced	SVW RE	–	13	349	11	.42
South-west white-slipped	SOW WS	–	1	13	1	–
Micaceous grey	MIC GW	TF5	21	261	18	.45
Malvernian rock-tempered	MAL RO	TF19	18	535	16	.49
Dorset Black-burnished ware	DOR BB1	TF4	77	1393	61	2.59
Lower Nene colour-coated	LNV CC	–	1	7	1	–
Oxford red colour-coated	OXF CC	–	8	105	8	.05
Oxford whiteware mortaria	OXF WHM	TF9w	2	66	2	.12
Midlands shell-tempered	ROB SH	TF22	8	143	8	.20
Total			**482**	**11807**	**389**	**9.52**

utilitarian bowls or dishes (19%). Malvernian wares are present as jars imitating Black-burnished ware types and lids. Severn Valley wares provide the majority of other forms, mostly tankards (17%), but including rarer flagons or handled jars (Fig. 7, nos 3–4). Such forms are known from Gloucester (Rawes 1982, fig. 2, nos 1–5) and among the kiln groups at Newland Hopfields, Worcestershire (Evans *et al*. 2000, fig. 19). Finewares are largely restricted to open forms, including for the earlier Roman period samian forms Drag. 18/31 and a fine greyware bowl (Fig. 7, no. 5) which is similar to a vessel from Home Farm, Bishop's Cleeve (Timby 1998, fig. 7, no. 20), and for the late Roman period Oxfordshire colour-coated ware bowls. A single Oxfordshire funnel-necked beaker of Young (1977) type C23 was recovered. Mortaria, which are confined to Oxfordshire whiteware types in Phase 4, are poorly represented in the assemblage. Evidence for use occurs in the form of sooting or burnt food residues on jars in Dorset Black-burnished ware and Malvernian wares. Additionally a number of Severn valley ware vessels, including handled jar no. 4, exhibit white limey internal residues, almost certainly produced through extended storage of water.

The assemblage is compositionally similar to larger groups from West Drive, Chelt-

Table 2: Quantification of the Period 1 pottery by phase

Phase	1			2			3			4		
Fabrics	EVEs	Est. vess.	%Est. vess.	EVEs	Est. vess.	%Est vess.	EVEs	Est. vess.	%Est vess.	EVEs	Est. vess.	%Est. vess.
LEZ SA2	–	–	–	–	4	1.8	–	1	1.1	–	1	3.8
BAT AM1	–	–	–	–	1	0.4	–	–	–	–	–	–
SAV GT	.10	1	3.7	–	–	–	–	–	–	–	–	–
LOC GT	–	9	33.3	.07	2	0.9	–	–	–	–	1	3.8
LOC GW	–	–	–	.10	6	2.6	–	10	10.8	–	1	3.8
OX CS	.50	1	3.7	–	–	–	–	–	–	–	–	–
LOC OX	–	–	–	–	3	1.3	–	2	2.2	–	–	–
SVW ET	–	–	–	0.55	13	5.8	–	2	2.2	–	–	–
SVW OX	.16	11	40.7	2.95	130	57.8	.67	36	38.7	.10	9	34.6
SVW RE	–	–	–	.36	8	3.6	–	2	2.2	.06	1	3.8
SOW WS	–	–	–	–	–	–	–	1	1.1	–	–	–
MIC GW	–	1	3.7	.08	8	3.6	.37	8	8.6	–	1	3.8
MAL RO	.06	1	3.7	.37	13	5.8	.06	1	1.1	–	1	3.8
DOR BB1	.15	3	11.1	1.82	35	15.6	.62	20	21.5	–	2	7.7
LNV CC	–	–	–	–	–	–	–	–	–	–	1	3.8
OXF CC	–	–	–	–	–	–	.05	6	6.5	–	4	15.4
OXF WHM	–	–	–	–	–	–	.12	2	2.2	–	–	–
ROB SH	–	–	–	–	2	0.9	–	2	2.2	.10	4	15.4
Total	**0.97**	**27**	–	**6.30**	**225**	–	**1.89**	**93**	–	**0.26**	**26**	–

enham and Home Farm, Bishop's Cleeve (Timby 2002; 1998, 126–8). The peak period of activity at each of these sites would on the basis of the pottery appear to be in the 2nd to 3rd centuries AD, with diminishing evidence for pottery use thereafter. Of greatest note at St James's is the evidence, largely absent at the other two sites, for a continuation of activity into the second half of the 4th century AD and after. A single bodysherd of organic-tempered pottery was recovered from Period 2 pit 2644, together with sherds of late Roman pottery including Midlands shell-tempered ware. The fabric of the organic-tempered sherd is similar to material from West Drive and Bishop's Cleeve, and is broadly dateable to the period between the 5th and 8th centuries (Timby 2002, 93; 1998, 134).

Site status is difficult to assess with a small group such as this. Lower status, at least for the earlier Roman period, might be reflected in the scarcity of samian and its occurrence as undecorated forms. There is an emphasis on utilitarian forms which may reflect lower status overall, as is also suggested by the use of a lead staple, of the type more often seen on samian vessels, to repair a Severn Valley ware bowl (Fig. 7, no. 6).

Chronology of Period 1

Phase 1. The small quantities of pottery which relate to Phase 1 are suggestive of activity extending from the mid or later 1st century AD to at least the later 2nd century. The absence of the hand-made Malvernian wares which are indicative of mid 1st century AD activity elsewhere in the region is significant. The earliest elements present, which probably date to the middle of the 1st century AD, consist of body sherds in 'Belgic'-type grogged fabrics from the pits and ditch 2897. A similar date, or one possibly extending into the early 2nd century, is probable for a ring-necked flagon in cream-slipped fabric from 2896 (Fig. 7, no. 1) and Savernake ware from 2897 (Fig. 7, no. 2). Groups from pit 3016 and ditches 2891 and 3015 are later and compositionally similar to groups from Phase 2. Dateable elements include 2nd to 3rd-century AD Severn Valley ware tankards and a Dorset Black-burnished ware jar of mid 2nd to mid 3rd-century AD date.

Phase 2: Larger quantities of pottery were recovered from features ascribed to this phase than for Phase 1. The largest groups, including those from ditches 2127 and 2134 are dominated by Severn Valley wares, almost to the exclusion of other types. Forms include 2nd/3rd-century AD tankards, handled-jars and bowls. Quantities of Dorset Black-burnished ware are moderately abundant and in a Gloucestershire context probably date to the 2nd century AD or later. This fabric is abundant in a large group of 99 sherds from ditch 2134, together with Severn Valley ware and wheel-thrown Malvernian wares. A mid or later 3rd-century AD date for this group is suggested by large sherds from a Dorset Black-burnished ware jar with obtuse-angled lattice decoration. Somewhat earlier dating, probably from the later 2nd century, is likely for much of the remaining material from this group, which includes Central Gaulish samian, a carinated bowl in a black-sandy fabric and a Severn Valley tankard with burnished lattice decoration.

Phase 3: Severn Valley ware is less dominant in Phase 3 compared with Phase 2, and Dorset Black-burnished ware and micaceous greywares are correspondingly more prevalent. New types present in the phase include Oxfordshire whiteware mortaria and colour-coated wares, and local brown colour-coated wares, the latter two of which are unlikely to be present in the region before *c.* AD 270/300. Dorset Black-burnished ware provides further markers for a date after *c.* AD 250/70 in the form of late-style jars (Gillam 1976, type 10–14) and flanged bowls (ibid., type 45–9).

Phase 4. Phase 4 produced small quantities of pottery, some of which is clearly residual. Composition is broadly comparable to the preceding phase. Most significant is the quantity of Midlands shell-tempered ware, a type which in this region rises to prominence only in the second half of the 4th century AD.

Catalogue of illustrated sherds (Fig. 7)

1   Ring-necked flagon, fabric OX CS. Period 1, Phase 1 ditch 2896.
2   Jar, fabric SAV GT. Period 1, Phase 1 ditch 2897.
3   Large flagon, fabric SVW OX. Period 1, Phase 2 ditch 2134.
4   Handled jar, fabric SVW OX. Period 1, Phase 2 ditch 2134.
5   Bowl with downward angled flange, fabric LOC GW. Period 1, Phase 2 ditch 2127.
6   Large flanged bowl with lead rivet repair. Fabric SVW OX. Period 1, Phase 2 ditch 2127.
7   Flanged bowl. Fabric ROB SH. Period 1, Phase 4 ditch 2903.

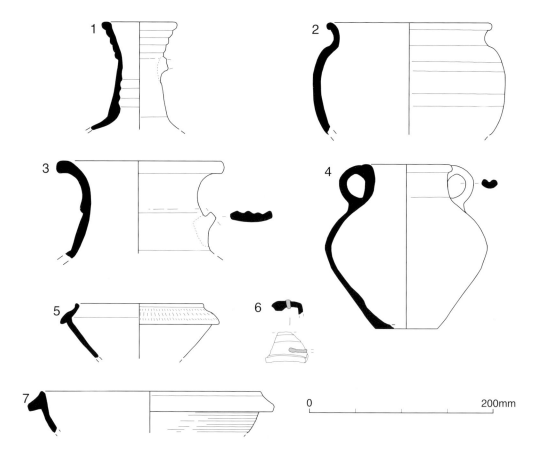

Fig. 7:   Roman pottery (scale 1:4)

Worked flint, by E.R. McSloy

Worked flint comprises 19 pieces (148g) all of which was residual in Roman or later features. Of greatest note within this assemblage are ten pieces of probable Mesolithic date. This small group include two small bladelet cores; a 'keeled' flake from a blade core 70mm in length; a possible burin, and five (broken) blades or bladelets, including one with a small area of re-touch. Core fragments and a number of the blades show evidence of preparatory platform abrasion. One blade exhibits clear signs of soft-hammer percussion as a low diffuse bulb and lipped 'butt'. All putative Mesolithic pieces exhibit patination to varying degrees, but mostly as deep white or yellowish discolouration. Few pieces retain any areas of cortex, although one of the bladelet cores clearly derived from a small well-worn pebble, which indicates some exploitation of gravel sources.

The remaining pieces comprise mainly secondary and some primary flake removals which, significantly, are unpatinated or only lightly patinated. A later Neolithic or Bronze Age date is likely for this material, which demonstrates far less control compared to the Mesolithic group. Direct evidence for late Neolithic activity is present in the form of a

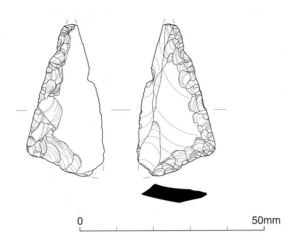

0   50mm

Fig. 8:   Flint transverse arrowhead (scale 1:1)

well-made and only slightly damaged arrowhead of transverse type (Fig. 8). The presence of fully cortical flakes demonstrates some primary reduction in the area, apparently using good quality chalk flint, clearly from outside the region.

1   (Fig. 8) 'British oblique'-type transverse arrowhead (Green 1980, fig. 38). Rolled condition with some damage to tip and 'barb'. Dark brown flint. Length 40mm; width 21mm. Period 1, phase 1 ditch 2891.

Worked stone, by E.R. McSloy with identifications by F. Roe

Small quantities of Old Red Sandstone roofing tile, which most probably originated from the Forest of Dean, were recovered from three contexts. Details of this material are available in the archive. Other worked stone of Roman date is restricted to a single rotary quern fragment from Phase 3 ditch 2894. The quern fragment, of Upper Old Red series conglomerate sandstone, had a slightly convex grinding surface and a small central perforation. The diameter of the quern was 370mm with a thickness of 85mm at the centre decreasing to 40mm at the edge. The source for this quern is also likely to have been the Forest of Dean area, approximately 20km to the south-west. As such this item fits the regional pattern for procurement, typical throughout the Roman period and reflected strongly in the much larger group of querns from West Drive, Cheltenham (Shaffrey 2002, 99; 2006). The form is typically Roman.

The only other stone object was from post-medieval context 2423 (not illustrated). It is lozenge shaped, with a hemispherical bulge on one face. This object almost certainly represents a spoon mould and probably dates to the 18th or 19th centuries. The stone type is uncertain but is probably lias.

THE BIOLOGICAL EVIDENCE

Human skeletal remains, by Louise Loe

The remains of one adult skeleton from grave 2881 were examined. Full osteological and palaeopathological analysis was carried out on the skeleton to determine, where possible, the age, sex and stature of the individual, record the presence of any discontinuous traits and to identify any evidence for bony abnormality or pathology. Full details of the methods adopted for analysis, and detailed results, are contained in the archive. Due to the fragmentary nature of the remains it was not possible to calculate the stature of this individual and little information could be derived from an analysis of dental health.

Approximately 45% of the skeleton had survived. Skull, mandible, torso and limbs were all present to some degree although in general they were all fragmented. The bones were in a fair condition with some abrasion to the cortical surfaces of long bones and minimal damage to joint surfaces. The remains of at least three carpal bones of a young child were also recorded. These had been recovered from the fill of the grave along with other bone fragments belonging to the adult skeleton.

Sex and age

The most reliable features used to sex skeletons are those that relate to the skull and the pelvis. When these bones are present, sex can be determined with 80–90% accuracy (Brothwell 1981). In this instance, none of these features had survived making sex determination difficult. In general, the remains represent a gracile, small-boned individual whose features tended towards the female range of expression. On their own these are not reliable indicators of sex and therefore this observation can only be regarded as approximate.

Age was assigned to the skeleton by observing the degree of wear on the molars and matching this with one of the age categories given by Brothwell (1981). For this individual, two right mandibular molars (2nd and 3rd) and one left maxillary molar (3rd) had survived. Although this technique is more reliable if all molars (12 in total) are present, it was concluded that this individual was between 25 and 35 years of age. In addition to this, the epiphysis of the medial right clavicle was fusing or had just fused at the time of death suggesting an age of about 20 to 30 years. No other age indicators had survived among the remains of this skeleton.

Non-metric traits

Non-metric or discontinuous morphological traits are discrete variants in the morphology of the skeleton. They occur both cranially, such as in the form of extra bones within the cranial sutures, and post cranially, such as an extra foramina in the humerus. The skeleton was examined for 14 cranial and eight post-cranial traits. These are detailed in the archive and are among the most commonly scored traits in skeletal populations. These were scored as; trait present (P), trait not present (0) and no data (–). Only five sites survived for scoring and of these two traits were present: a septal aperture on the left humerus and one wormian bone in the lambdoid suture. These traits are commonly observed in populations of this date and type (Brothwell 1981).

Bone abnormality and pathology

Periostitis was observed on the visceral surfaces on one left rib fragment and 15 small unsided rib fragments. Periostitis is an inflammatory condition that affects the layer of soft tissue that overlies the surface of bone (the periostium) in life. It typically appears on the skeleton as pitting, longitudinal striations and plaque-like new bone. This is a non-specific condition that is most commonly seen on the shafts of the tibias and can occur as a result of something as minor as varicose veins or as severe as tuberculosis. In this case the most likely diagnosis is inflammation resulting from a respiratory disease of unknown aetiology. It is not possible to say what caused this condition, nor is it possible to comment on its severity or say whether it contributed to cause of death.

Animal bone, by Sylvia Warman

The animal bone assemblage was reviewed at assessment stage by A. Barber. Further details on the methods used are contained in the archive. Although no further work was recommended beyond assessment the Roman material merits a brief discussion. Table 3 details the proportions of each of the species identified. The identifiable material is dominated by cattle, with much smaller numbers of dog, pig, sheep and horse. The only non-mammal bone identified was a single chicken bone (a tarso-metatarsus with part of the spur remaining, indicating the bone was from a male individual). This small assemblage appears to represent butchers' waste rather than domestic waste and contributes to the data set on Roman animal husbandry in Cheltenham begun by the West Drive report (Baxter 2002). The dominance of cattle at this site is even greater than that represented there.

Table 3: Animal bne from Roman (Period 1) deposits

	Taxon	No. fragments
Cattle	*Bos taurus*	270
Sheep/goat	*Ovis/Capra*	9
Pig	*Sus scrofa*	13
Dog	*Canis amiliaris*	17
Horse	*Equus caballus*	8
Chicken	*Gallus gallus*	1
Large mammal		126
Sheep-sized mammal		98
Indeterminate		573
Total		**1115**

Plant remains, by E. Hutchens

Environmental samples were taken from a variety of features and were processed at assessment stage. Only low quantities of charred plant remains and molluscs were recovered, and this material has little potential to assist in the reconstruction of environmental conditions on the site. Full details are contained in the archive. Sample 1 from ditch 2507 is most noteworthy, seeming to contain chaff parts from the early stages of crop processing. The remaining samples produced only small quantities of charred remains including common weed seeds and cereals including oat (*Avena sativa*), rye (*Secale cereale*), buttercup (*Ranunculus*) and nettle (*Urtica*).

DISCUSSION

The recovery of a small assemblage of Mesolithic flint artefacts is of some interest, although a lack of cut features which could be associated with these finds renders further interpretation difficult. Mesolithic activity in Gloucestershire is known almost entirely from artefact scatters identified during fieldwalking or (as in this case) from the excavation of later sites (Saville 1984, 69). Even large-scale projects have not produced much in the way of Mesolithic material. For instance fieldwork on the route of the 27km-long Wormington to Tirley pipeline near the Gloucestershire and Worcestershire border found only a single posthole of possible Mesolithic date and a handful of contemporary flints (Coleman *et al.* 2006, 29, 57–8). The flintwork nevertheless testifies to prehistoric activity along the bank of the Chelt, although nothing else has been found in the present project to provide any further information or context on the putative Neolithic portal dolmen supposedly found nearby (see Introduction).

The earliest phase of Romano-British activity dates from the mid/late 1st century AD and comprised ditches and pits. It is probable that some features dating to this phase have been obscured or recut by those of subsequent phases. The alignment of the Phase 1 ditches in the western part of the site is followed by a Phase 2 ditch immediately to the east. The absence of Malvernian ware from the site indicates that this activity dates to after the mid 1st century AD, and no pre-Conquest origin for the fieldsystem is suggested on current evidence. The establishment of agricultural activity in this part of Cheltenham is therefore likely to be broadly contemporary with the foundation of the *colonia* at Gloucester, 10km to the south-west, at the end of the 1st century AD. The majority of Romano-British features dated to the 2nd to 3rd centuries AD and comprised ditches forming an irregular grid system. One of these ditches contained chaff from the early stages of crop processing, and the bone assemblage appears to represent butchery waste, primarily that of cattle. At the centre of the site a number of ditches appeared to form a rough herring-bone pattern converging on ditch 2127 which drained south-westwards towards the valley of the Chelt. Development of the field system continued into the later 3rd and 4th century AD with recutting of the existing ditches and the construction of new ones. Ditch 2134 may have continued into the eastern part of the site, but was recut by ditches 2506 and 2507. By the mid to late 4th century AD most ditches had largely silted up and only a few new ones were dug within a restricted part of the site. Two graves were also found in this area, just within the south-eastern corner of the 2nd to 3rd-century AD field ditches. One of the graves can be dated to the late 4th century AD and by inference the other is likely to be of a similar date. They do not appear to be part of a formal cemetery, rather their dispersed nature and probable association with a major ditch intersection suggests a more informal pattern of burial commonly identified at the fringes of Romano-British rural settlements (Pearce 1999, 151). In a local context similar burials have been found at and Rudgeway Lane, Walton Cardiff and Frocester (see report earlier in this volume; Price 2000). The single sherd of post-Roman pottery is tantalising evidence for activity continuing in the vicinity into the 5th century AD or later, and joins the growing list of sites in this part of the Severn Vale where this fabric has been recognised (for instance at Frocester; West Drive, Cheltenham, and Bishop's Cleeve: Timby 2000, 137–8; 2002, 93; 1998; 2007). We may also note that the fieldsystem excavated at West Drive has a very similar chronology to that found here (Catchpole 2002).

The discoveries made at this site provide firm evidence for a nearby Romano-British settlement which presumably lay to the north or east (evaluation to the west revealed negative results; Fig. 1). The late 1st-century AD date for the start of activity makes it unlikely that the fields were associated with a villa house at such an early date, although it is possible that this was added later to a pre-existing farmstead as at Frocester and probably Bishop's Cleeve (Holbrook 2006, 109). If this was so, however, the house is unlikely to have lain adjacent to this site as only a single fragment of Roman tile (*imbrex*) was recovered from the ditches in a 3rd or 4th-century AD context. Indeed the reduced activity in the mid-late 4th century AD apparent here might have been as a consequence of changing patterns of agricultural production associated with the creation of a villa somewhere in the wider vicinity. The presence of one or more villas in the Cheltenham area would not be unexpected as such settlements in the Severn Vale tend to favour the spreads of fan gravels and wind blown sand in preference to heavier lias clays where non-villa settlement is more prevalent (Holbrook 2004, 88). The work at this site represents a start in understanding the nature of Romano-British activity adjacent to the river Chelt, and further discoveries will doubtless be made in this part of Cheltenham in the future which will clarify the context of the fieldsystem.

ACKNOWLEDGEMENTS

The evaluation was supervised by Laurent Coleman, assisted by Jon Hart, and managed by Neil Holbrook, Geoff Potter and Graeme Walker. The excavation was directed by Laurent Coleman, assisted by Tim Havard, and managed by Martin Watts. The post-excavation process was managed by Martin Watts and all phases of work were monitored by Charles Parry of Gloucestershire County Council Archaeology Service. The fieldwork and post-excavation was funded by the John Lewis Partnership and the authors would particularly like to thank Mark Owen of main contractors Costain and Adrian Hopkins of the John Lewis Partnership for their interest in our work. The report was edited for publication by Neil Holbrook and the illustrations are by Peter Moore. The archive will be deposited at Cheltenham Art Gallery and Museum under accession number 1999.207.

BIBLIOGRAPHY

Baxter, I. 2002 'The animal bones', in Catchpole 2002, 96–8
BGS 1988 *1:50000 series England and Wales Sheet 216 Tewkesbury Solid and Drift Geology*
Brothwell, D. 1981 *Digging up bones* London, British Museum (Natural History)
CA 2005 *St George's Place, Cheltenham, Gloucestershire. Archaeological evaluation* CA unpublished report no. **05169**
CAT 2001 *The Catholic School of St Gregory the Great, Cheltenham, Gloucestershire: archaeological evaluation* CAT unpublished report no. **01043**
Catchpole, T. 2002 'Excavations at West Drive, Cheltenham, Gloucestershire 1997–9', *Trans. Bristol Gloucestershire Archaeol. Soc.* **120**, 89–102
Coleman, L., 1999 *St James's development Cheltenham, Gloucestershire: archaeological evaluation* CAT unpublished report no. **991109**

Coleman, L. and Watts, M. 2001 'A Romano-British field system at Cheltenham: evidence from excavations at St James's car park', *Glevensis* **34**, 67–71

Coleman, L., Hancocks, A. and Watts, M. 2006 *Four sites by the Carrant Brook and River Isbourne, Gloucestershire and Worcestershire: excavations on the Wormington to Tirley pipeline 2000* Cotswold Archaeology Monograph **2**, Cirencester

Darvill, T. 2004 *Long barrows of the Cotswolds* Stroud, Tempus

Evans, C., Jones, L. and Ellis, P. 2000 *Severn Valley ware production at Newland Hopfields* BAR British Series **313**, Oxford, British Archaeological Reports

Gillam, J.P. 1976 'Coarse fumed ware in North Britain', *Glasgow Archaeol. J.* **4**, 57–80

Goding, J. 1863 *Norman's history of Cheltenham* Cheltenham

Green, H. 1980 *The flint arrowheads of the British Isles* BAR British Series **75**, Oxford, British Archaeological Reports

Holbrook, N. 2004 'Romano-British' in G.T. Walker, A. Thomas and C. Bateman 'Bronze Age and Romano-British sites south-east of Tewkesbury: evaluation and excavation 1991–7', *Trans. Bristol Gloucestershire Archaeol. Soc.* **122**, 87–90

Holbrook, N. 2006 'The Roman period', in N. Holbrook and J. Juřica (eds) *Twenty-five years of archaeology in Gloucestershire. A review of new discoveries and new thinking in Gloucestershire, South Gloucestershire and Bristol 1979–2004* Bristol Gloucestershire Archaeol. Rep. **3**, Cirencester, Cotswold Archaeology, 97–131

Pearce, J., 1999 'The dispersed dead: preliminary observations on burial and settlement space in rural Britain', in P. Baker, C. Forcey, S. Jundi and R. Witcher (eds) *Proceedings of the eighth annual theoretical Roman archaeology conference, Leicester 1998* Oxford, Owbow Books, 151–62

Price, E. 2000 *Frocester. A Romano-British settlement, its antecedents and successors* Stonehouse, Gloucester and District Archaeological Research Group; 2 vol

Rawes, B., 1974 'Some aspects of the archaeology of the borough of Cheltenham', *Glevensis* **8**, 19–22.

Rawes, B. 1982 'Gloucester Severn valley ware', *Trans. Bristol Gloucestershire Archaeol. Soc.* **100**, 33–46

Saville, A., 1981 'Cheltenham', in R.H. Leech (ed.) *Historic towns in Gloucestershire* CRAAGS Survey **8**, Bristol, CRAAGS, 8–11.

Saville, A. 1984 'Palaeolithic and Mesolithic evidence from Gloucestershire', in A. Saville (ed.) *Archaeology in Gloucestershire* Cheltenham, Cheltenham Art Gallery and Museums and Bristol and Gloucestershire Archaeological Society, 59–79

Shaffrey, R. 2002 'Catalogue of worked stone', in Catchpole 2002, 99

Shaffrey, R. 2006 *Grinding and milling: a study of Romano-British rotary querns and millstones made from old red sandstone* BAR British Series **409**, Oxford, British Archaeological Reports

Timby, J. 1998 'Pottery' in Barber and Walker 1998, 134

Timby, J. 2000 'Pottery' in Price 2000, 125–62

Timby, J. 2002 'The pottery', in Catchpole 2002, 92–6

Timby, J. 2007 'Pottery fabrics', in J. Lovell, J. Timby, G. Wakeham and M.J. Allen 'Iron Age to Saxon farming settlement at Bishop's Cleeve, Gloucestershire: excavations south of Church Road, 1998 and 2004', *Trans. Bristol Gloucestershire Archaeol. Soc.* **125**, 95–129

Tomber, R. and Dore, J. 1998 *The national Roman fabric reference collection: a handbook* London, MoLAS monograph **2**, Museum of London

Wain, I. 1997 *St James Station site, Cheltenham: archaeological desk based assessment* Oxford Archaeological Unit unpublished report

Wills, J. 1987 'Chester Walk, Cheltenham', *Trans. Bristol Gloucestershire Archaeol. Soc.* **105**, 243–4

Young, C J 1977 *Oxfordshire Roman pottery* BAR British Series **43**, Oxford, British Archaeological Reports